Fen Country Christmas

EDWARD STOREY

Illustrated by
Helen Hale

ROBERT HALE · LONDON

© *Edward Storey 1995*
First published in Great Britain 1995

ISBN 0 7090 5511 0

Robert Hale Limited
Clerkenwell House
Clerkenwell Green
London EC1R 0HT

2 4 6 8 10 9 7 5 3 1

Photoset in Palatino by
Derek Doyle & Associates, Mold, Clwyd.
Printed in Great Britain by
St Edmundsbury Press Ltd, Bury St Edmunds, Suffolk.
Bound by WBC Book Manufacturers Limited,
Bridgend, Mid-Glamorgan.

It was always said of him that he knew how to keep Christmas well, if any man alive possessed the knowledge …

Charles Dickens

Gradually there gathered the felling of expectation. Christmas was coming. In the shed, at nights, a secret candle was burning …

D.H. Lawrence

To perceive Christmas through its wrapping becomes more difficult each year …

E.B. White

for

JOHN and SYLVIA

Contents

Introduction

1

There was a time when Christmas for me began in August and my neighbours were puzzled to hear me at the piano playing *In the Bleak Midwinter* when there was a heatwave outside.

The reason for this was that for several years, whilst working for the local education authority, I was involved in helping to organize the schools' carol services which were then held in Peterborough Cathedral.

Although these would not take place until December, the preparations had to begin much earlier. Schools needed to know fairly soon in the autumn term which carols they would have to start learning. There were always two, sometimes three, services with about two thousand children at the Primary Schools' Service and at least a thousand at the Secondary Schools' Service.

The children arrived in convoys of buses – single-deckers, double-deckers, buses out of the museums, town buses, country buses, all arriving like an invasion force into the peaceful cathedral precincts. Occasionally it snowed but mostly it rained and we had to imagine the bleakness described in Christina Rossetti's poem.

My two colleagues and I had been busy for days before the event, hauling in hundreds of extra chairs borrowed from the schools, arranging rehearsals for choirs and readers, keeping on the right side of the vergers, and getting the service sheets printed in time. The printing was done for us by a small, dynamic Polish Jew who knew the carols better than we did and often corrected our errors. He had survived some very dangerous flying missions during the war and now applied his energies to running a printing works and to selling greetings cards.

But, before any of these final preparations could be achieved, the carols and readings had to be chosen, discussed and agreed upon, which is why my neighbours heard me crooning 'frosty winds made moan' while they sweltered in soaring summer temperatures, thinking perhaps that I had gone a little, if not completely, mad.

There were always the old favourites which had to be included every year otherwise we would have had a mutiny on our hands – *Once in Royal David's City* and *O Come all ye Faithful* went in unopposed. Others had to be fought for, such as *The Coventry Carol* and *In the Bleak Midwinter*. 'Can't we give them a rest' someone would ask. 'They're so mournful and the children loathe them.'

Even more thorny than the choice of carols was the complicated seating arrangements in the cathedral. Where possible we worked on a rotation basis so that schools which were pushed to the back of the long nave, or tucked away in one of the draughty transepts one year, were more favourably placed the next. It wasn't easy because some rural schools had sixty pupils and some of the city schools more than six hundred.

But they were wonderful occasions and may help to explain why, more than thirty years later, I am still imbued with a love of Christmas and the sound of carol singing, even when the commercial side of it all rouses my impatience and occasionally my temper. What I try to do then is remember the solo voice of a boy or girl echoing through that vast building, or recall a children's choir singing *Away in a Manger*, and I am back to where all those shining faces were, once upon a time, and peace is restored on earth again, and there is goodwill towards men.

2

Looking back over the years it is impossible to say which Christmasses have given me the greatest joy, or have produced the most lasting memories. After those early

childhood excitements of hanging up my stocking and waiting for Father Christmas, I think my first experiences of carol singing with the chapel choir come close. For me it was an adventure which gave me the chance of being out late at night without my parents there to keep an eye on me. Not that I could get away with too much mischief because the choir was made up almost entirely of aunts, uncles, cousins, second cousins and neighbours. But there was still plenty of fun as we went from house to house, or from pub to pub, where we were sometimes asked inside to sing to the customers. We also knew at which houses we would be offered mince pies or sausage-rolls, at which ones we could expect a generous contribution to our collection box and, equally, which ones to avoid.

We not only had to compete with the other chapel choirs but with the town band, whose warm, glowing sounds could be heard streets away and always thrilled more than any choir. It was one of the special pleasures my father had as a young man. He loved to go out carol playing on Christmas Eve and spoke of it often in his last years when memory was a way of life. The band stayed out until past midnight, when they felt justified in playing *Christians, awake! Salute the happy morn*. It would have been wrong to have played it sooner.

I remember that one year we went to sing to a widow who lived on the outskirts of the town. She used to attend our chapel but, since her husband's death, had not wanted to go out much. It was a beautiful, moonlit night and as I looked up at the sky I was aware that I was staring at a moon that was there before Bethlehem, before Herod or the Pharaohs, before Moses came down from the mountain or Adam was turned out of paradise. It did not spoil the Christmas story at all. Truth and fable take their place in a far greater scheme that we can always comprehend.

3

There have been those Christmasses too as an adult which add their own memories to the season – Christmasses without children or parties, when quietness was more important than noise and the company of a few better than crowds. The years pass and familiar faces are missing. Then other meanings take over.

Although all but two of my Christmasses have been spent in the Fens, those two exceptions stand out as very special ones. Both were in Salzburg and one included a Christmas Eve visit to the village of Oberndorf where the carol *Stille Nacht* was written in 1818.

We were apprehensive, thinking it would all be very commercialized and vulgar, for simplicity is always ruined the moment it becomes a spectacle. It would probably be far from a 'silent night, holy night' and, as we approached the village, we thought our worst fears were to be confirmed. Coaches and cars lined the roadside, indicating that several hundred people were already there. But, as requested, they had left their vehicles and walked into the centre of the village to gather round the small church where the carol was first performed. The church, which is not the original one, cannot seat more than about sixty people, so the large congregation of over two thousand now stood shoulder to shoulder outside, waiting for the service to begin. There were Americans, Japanese, New Zealanders, French and German – all ready to share in the re-enactment of something that seemed too simple to be true. The village band played somewhere in the dark trees beyond the church and then the villagers arrived in their national costumes, many of them carrying lanterns or posies of flowers. At that moment the lights on the fir trees were switched on and the priest emerged from the interior of the church to explain how Joseph Mohr and Franz Gruber (the priest and organist at the time) had to devise some way of providing their congregation with music that Christmas because the church organ was so badly in need of repair it couldn't be played. Father Mohr suggested to his organist that he should accompany the singing on his guitar and also compose a simple hymn for the occasion. Franz Gruber said he could easily write a tune but would need some suitable words. The priest went home and, two hours later, presented Franz with the verses of *Stille Nacht, Heilige Nacht*. And so the now famous carol was born. As we listened to the rest of the story two young men – representing the composer and the priest – stepped out from the church and, with the original guitar accompaniment, began to sing. They sang the first two verses alone and we were all invited to sing the third verse in our own tongues – English, French, Italian, and possibly Japanese. As we did so the first few flakes of snow began to fall, settling on the trees, then on us. They fluttered like white moths round the villagers' lanterns and brought a breathless moment of magic to an already memorable night. The service ended, the priest gave the blessing, and the multi-racial, multi-denominational congregation quietly dispersed. There was no collection, no beggars, no commercialization, simply an over-powering sense of wonder and gratitude that this small part of Christmas had been left unspoilt. We had crossed the boundaries of disbelief, cynicism or fear. People went back to their cars, back to their homes, hotels, modern comforts and celebrations, and not one of them could have been untouched by that hour.

4

Whatever changes there have been in our beliefs, lifestyles or customs over recent years, there is still an unchangeable magic about Christmas that is irresistible. We get caught up in it whether we like it or not. We are drawn into its web of traditions, of present giving, carol singing, expense and frustration because part of it still has the power to make us believe, if only for a few days, that the world is going to be different.

'And is it true?' asks Sir John Betjeman in his poem *Christmas*. 'And is it true, this most tremendous tale of all?' It might be. We don't really know for sure because the facts have all been clouded by so many other beliefs, legends, superstitions and doubts, even by those whose livelihoods depend on the Nativity. Some experts also tell us that we have got the dates wrong and are several weeks out in our calculations. But does it matter? The message is more important today than the proof.

For many of us Christmas will always be associated with the remembrance of things past. And why not? A little healthy nostalgia never did any harm. There may be times when we should be wary of trusting our memories for, all too often, we see only what we want to see. But the past is frequently illuminated more by imagination than by memory. That is surely better than being indifferent to it.

None of us can escape the past any more than a kite can

escape the string on which its flying depends, unless of course the string is cut. Then the kite has no purpose.

To enjoy Christmas fully we have to suspend belief – or disbelief – and take what cannot be measured by any history books, sciences or creeds. We have to regain the pleasure of hearing a good story told round the fireside – and the better the story the more convinced by it we shall be.

Sadly, in an age of central-heating, television and computer-games, the hearth is no longer the focal point of our living-rooms that it once was. That change alone has almost eliminated the art of spontaneous storytelling and natural conversation. And where talk ceases, memories decay.

5

This collection of stories, essays and poems is a journey of the imagination as well as a record of fact. Its main purpose is to entertain. The essays are factual, the poems were written over many years, usually for carol services, and the stories (though loosely based on events which happened) are pure fiction in which place names have been changed and the characters are not meant to portray any known person, living or dead.

Although the stories all have the same geographical setting they will, I hope, appeal to readers unfamiliar with the fen country and its history for, in the end, their message is both simple and universal for this time of the year. It would be a loss if Christmas became no more than an ordinary, unmysterious Bank Holiday and I would like to think that we can still keep alive the spirit of the star and manger, the shepherds and wise men, the wonder and hope, even though some of the questions will always remain unanswered.

Above all, and for whatever reason, it is a time of celebration and we could do worse than remind ourselves of the lines from *Hamlet*:

> Some say that ever 'gainst that season comes
> Wherein our Saviour's birth is celebrated,

The bird of dawning singeth all night long ...
So hallow'd and so gracious is the time.

Finally, I wish to thank all those people who have shared their memories of Christmas with me and provided the background material for several of these chapters.

EDWARD STOREY
1994

1 Coincidence at Common Acre

Let me begin with the story of a retired farmer whom I met some years ago and whose memories of a certain Christmas impressed me so much that I have never forgotten them. His name was David Glassmoor and he had invited me to call one evening to look at his collection of early maps of the Fens. Later, as we sat having a drink, he told me of a strange coincidence that happened to him as a boy when he stayed one year with his grandparents:

I can still remember their house as clearly as if it had been my own home. It was the last house in the village before the road reached the fields, and was called 'Hollies End'. Most of the land then belonged to Mr Boucher, a prosperous farmer near Littleport. My grandfather had been his foreman for many years and as a favour was allowed to stay on in the house after he retired. That was more than sixty years ago, before the village of Common Acre was deserted and the house eventually pulled down to make way for an industrial estate. Everyone, of course, blamed the machines. First the binders and tractors, then the lorries, beet-lifters and combines that took over from the horses and old farm labourers. Soon fewer hands were needed on the land and people had to look elsewhere for work. In time the school closed, the grocery store was sold up, the pub lost its trade and the rest of the village was left to crumble away, too isolated and unattractive to appeal to urban people eager for a taste of the so-called idyllic country life.

17

My parents were among those who moved west to find work in Clayton, a small town twenty miles away that had grown up in the nineteenth century when bricks were the product of a new industry. With no transport of their own my parents seldom went back to the old village more than twice a year, which was usually at Easter and just before Christmas. A few years later there was no reason for going back at all.

My grandparents' house was a large, double-fronted one partly covered with Virginia Creeper. The rooms were spacious compared with those of our terraced house at home and I was always fascinated by a stained-glass window on the landing, half-way up the stairs. It was of a Dutch landscape with a windmill, a boy in clogs, and a dyke that stretched towards a setting sun. The house originally had four bedrooms but the smallest was later converted into a bathroom, a luxury which gave my grandmother immense pride.

She had made up her mind in October that she wanted all the family together again for Christmas, as if she had some premonition that it would be the last gathering of its kind at 'Hollies End'. No one wanted to deny her that wish so we all agreed to go. I was ten and my sister Laura was eight. My Uncle Jack had agreed to fetch us in his car on Christmas Eve so that we didn't have to bother about local buses, which were infrequent and unreliable. What with our suit-cases and parcels the morning had all the excitement of going on a summer holiday to the seaside, but it was a cold day with a threat of snow. Some of the fields were already flooded and frozen. 'Another night or two of frost,' said Jack to my father, 'and we'll be skating. Do you still have your Welney Runners?'

My father had been a good skater when he was a young man and some villages prided themselves on the skates made by their local blacksmiths. My father's had long since gone rusty hanging in our shed. 'I've not bin on a pair of skates since I left Common Acre,' he replied. 'I doubt if I could even stand up straight on the ice now, let alone skate.'

My uncle turned to me. 'What about you David?' he asked. 'You can't come from the Fens and not know 'ow to skate. That wouldn't go down at all well.'

My father, who had a habit of speaking for the rest of the family, said 'All 'e's interested in is football.' It was not the answer I would have given, but I did not contradict him. Some of my friends at school were able to skate and I wished to join them, but I knew there was no point in asking my parents for skates, not yet, especially as my father had only recently got his job back after having an accident in the brickyards ...

David Glassmoor poured us each another scotch and continued:

When we arrived at 'Hollies End' the Christmas tree in the front room window had already been lit and there was a bunch of mistletoe hanging in the porch. Uncle Jack drove us round to the back door and helped us to carry our luggage into the house, where grandma was in the kitchen making pastry. She acknowledged our presence but went on with her work, telling us to make ourselves at home. 'You know where everything is and which bedrooms you can have, so help yourselves. John's out with the dog and should be getting me some more greenery.'

Uncle Jack winked at my father. 'I bet 'e's popped down to *The Three Pickerels* for a pint. Perhaps we should go and look for 'im.'

Now as far as I know grandad was not really much of a drinker and went down to the pub as much to smoke his pipe as he did to have a beer. Grandma didn't like him smoking in the house, particularly as his brand of tobacco was a very strong, aromatic one which she always claimed was a mixture of dried cow-dung and twitch.

We had only been there for about ten minutes when he, and the dog Shep, came in with a large bundle of holly and ivy. Grandad placed it on the table. 'There you are, old girl! Nothing like living in a jungle when you're trying to eat your Christmas pudden.'

By early evening every picture, mirror and wall-clock was draped in evergreens, adding contrast to the gaudy, home-made paper chains which were looped from corner to corner of the high ceiling.

Laura and I played with Shep until it was supper time, guessing about some of the presents we thought we would get from Father Christmas. I already knew he didn't exist and that the pillow-cases were filled by our parents, but Laura still believed in him and I wasn't about to spoil her excitement.

When we had finished our meal grandad filled his pipe and said he was going to take the dog for a short walk. I asked him if I could go too. 'Put your coat and scarf on,' said mother. 'We don't want you going down with pneumonia again.'

The outside of the house was as interesting to me as the inside. As well as the yard, with its old pump and rusty plough, there was an overgrown paddock, some sheds and a large barn where grandma kept some hens and Mr Boucher still stabled his horse. I remembered that the previous time I had stayed with my grandparents it was summer and I had spent most of my time outdoors, enjoying the long, light evenings and listening to the skylarks in the nearby fields – far more than you'll hear today … Now, when we stepped outside, it was very dark and very frosty. It took a few seconds for me to get used to the immense blackness. I noticed how still and quiet it was. There were a few lights down in the village but over the Fens there was a deep, mysterious silence. You could almost feel it.

We walked along the edge of a field and I stopped to look up at the sky. It was flooded with sparkling stars. I stood staring at them, wondering just how many thousands there were. My grandfather was watching me. 'Do you know what all those stars are called, boy?'

'Only some,' I said. 'Do they all have names?'

He pointed to the different constellations and told me what they were. He was not an educated man but he knew all kinds of things like the phases of the moon, the times of high tides and low tides, the changes in the weather and where the birds would build their nests each year. He loved nature and felt very much part of it. 'On a night like this,' he said, 'it makes you feel that you could pluck one of those stars right out of the sky.'

I noticed there was one star much brighter than the rest. 'What's that big one over there?' I asked.

He turned his eyes from Orion and looked towards the east. There was a moment or two of silence as he drew on his pipe and then exhaled a long, deep breath, as if he was buying time. 'You've got me beat there, boy. I just can't believe that I've never noticed that one afore. P'raps it's only visible late at night.'

I was quick to point out that it wasn't very late but he made no comment. 'Perhaps it's a comet,' I suggested, boastingly.

'Maybe,' he said, as he called Shep. 'It's time we got back to the house, otherwise you won't wake up in the morning to see what Father Christmas has left you.' I scoffed at that remark and said I was too old for all that nonsense.

David Glassmoor chuckled quietly to himself before saying:

It's funny, isn't it … there was something special about going to bed on Christmas Eve in someone else's house those days and, in a way, if only for my sister Laura's sake, I found myself wanting to believe in Father Christmas again, just to find out whether or not he knew where we were that year. But there was no fear of not waking up early next morning. Before dawn broke we were delving into our packed pillow-cases to see what we had received. One of my presents was certainly unexpected. I thought at first it was a pair of slippers in a shoe-box until I felt the weight. But when I removed the layers of tissue-paper I found something much more interesting – a pair of Welney Runners, you know, the sort that you strapped on to your boots. I couldn't believe my eyes and read the card again: 'When you can skate as well as Charlie Tubbs I'll buy you a pair of Norwegians – Happy Xmas, Uncle Jack.'

I wasn't sure who Charlie Tubbs was but my father said that he had once been a famous speed skater in the Fens and still held some of the records. 'I doubt if anyone else will ever skate as well as him,' he said, discouragingly.

We carried all our presents downstairs where the table was already laid for the traditional fen-country breakfast of pork pie, sausages, ham, bread and butter, pickles and dried fruit. The fire was blazing and grandad was twiddling the knobs of his wireless set, trying to find a programme of carols.

Later in the morning my aunts Hilda and Doris arrived with their husbands, Jack and Gordon. With them came our cousins – Betty, Peter, Jenny and Norman. I thought the house would explode with so many people and so much noise. My father helped grandad to serve the drinks – sherry, port or beer for the grown-ups, lemonade or cider for the children. An hour later the fourteen of us sat down to a Christmas dinner that needs no description from me for I'm sure that many similar ones were being served in the Fens that day. We certainly knew how to tuck in.

Afterwards, Uncle Jack came over to me and said, 'The ice is bearing on Lodden Fen. Would you like to try your skates?'

We drove along the river-bank until we came to a gate that led to a large field which was now a frozen lake. A dozen people were already out skating and I felt very nervous. Jack noticed and said, 'Don't worry, everybody's got to begin somewhere. You'll soon get the hang of it.' Then he took an old wooden chair from the back of the car and carried it on to the ice. He told me to hold on to it, like a walking-frame, until I got the feel of my skates. 'They're just an extension of your legs, so learn to relax. You can remember what it was like when you first learnt to ride a bike, can't you? Right then. If you can stay upright on two narrow wheels surely you can manage to do so on two blades of steel. At least you won't 'ave so far to fall.' It wasn't immediately successful. My skates frequently slipped from under me and the chair tipped over. But, by the end of the afternoon, I could make some progress and was sorry to see the winter light fading so quickly. Jack told me to sit on the chair while he unbuckled the straps and removed my skates, then we walked back to the car. A frosty mist was now creeping over the ice and there was a feeling of unreality in the air. In a way I already felt more grown up.

In the evening there was the usual programme of family games and entertainment before we all sat down to a supper of cold meats and pickles. Then grandad decided it was time to take Shep out for his last piddles, as he called it. Again, I asked if I could go with him and quickly fetched my coat and scarf. We walked through the yard, up to the headlands. It was another clear, cold night and I looked for the bright, nameless star. It was not in the same place as the night before but now shone more directly overhead, nearer the stars we did know. 'I think you may be right, David,' said my grandfather. 'That must be a comet – which explains why I couldn't tell you its name last night. Some of 'em, they say, only appear once every few hundred years, so you'd have thought they would have said something about it in the papers.'

Shep went running off in all directions, sniffing and panting as if he had picked up the scent of a fat rabbit. Then he began to bark. 'Why's he doing that?' I asked.

'Don't ask me, boy. Whatever it is it can't be very serious. I think at times 'e just lets 'is imagination run away with him.' We turned to walk back to the house.

'Do dogs have imaginations?' I asked.

'Why shouldn't they?' he said. 'We know they dream and what's a dream if it's not imagination.' Shep barked again and grandad whistled him to come to heel.

We reached the kitchen door and I raised the latch. The house felt so warm and bright after the darkness. My aunts were helping my mother to wash up and there were still games being played in the front room. Uncle Gordon was trying to play the piano and Uncle Jack was trying to sing, but I don't think it was the same piece of music. Peter and Norman were wrestling behind the sofa and it was nearly midnight before Laura and I were told to get ready for bed. 'See you in the morning, David,' shouted Jack from the door. 'Get your skates on …' He went off singing into the dark and I noticed that my father was smiling, perhaps enviously.

Well, Boxing Day can never quite match Christmas Day, can it! There are few secrets left, little anticipation, and no unexplained magic. It's just a repeat performance without the wonder. It had been arranged that we would all go to Aunt Hilda's for dinner and then go to Aunt Doris's for the evening and supper, where we expected there would be endless games of cards for the adults and mostly Ludo and Snakes and Ladders for the children, unless we could think of something more interesting while they were all engrossed in their whist.

From the moment I woke up on Boxing Day morning I knew there had been a change in the weather. The bedroom ceiling reflected a different whiteness from outside. I looked out and saw that everything was now covered with snow. It cloaked the shrubs, hedges, fences, farm implements and roof-tops with a soft white moss that dazzled even without sunlight. Only on the path that led through the yard to the barn could I see what looked like footprints. But these were already partly hidden by more recent snow and could have been made by the man who went to feed Mr Boucher's horse. There was no one else up when Laura and I crept downstairs to get some breakfast before going out to play with Shep in the snow. It was wonderful to step into such a silent, unspoilt world. The Fens looked even more expansive as they stretched towards a far distant horizon. It was like a land that had just been made. Shep leapt and rolled in the snow with great frenzy. Then he picked up a scent and suddenly started sniffing his way to the barn. We followed, eager to see what he might find. But there was nothing there, apart from the horse and grandma's hens roosting in the rafters, all looked quite unconcerned as we stared at them. Shep had jumped up on to some hay and was pawing away at it vigorously. I remembered his barking from the night before. We went over to see if there was something there after all. Laura took off her gloves and stooped down to touch the hay. 'It's warm,' she said. 'You feel.'

It was true. The hay was warm, as if someone had recently slept on it, perhaps more than one, for the whole area had a distinct feel and shape about it that was nowhere else in the barn. 'It must have been the horse,' I said, without thinking, 'or a fox.' Laura pointed to the horse that was tethered in its stall.

'It couldn't have been him, could it!' I had to agree. 'Perhaps it was a tramp,' I suggested, 'or a ghost.'

'Ghosts can't make things warm,' said Laura, knowingly. 'They don't have any blood.'

We watched Shep rummage in the hay for a bit and then, with an air of disappointment, he picked up a scent out of the barn and ran into the paddock. Again we followed, still speculating on what, or who, might have slept there during the night. 'Should we tell grandad?' my sister asked. I told her we shouldn't mention it to anyone.

'You know what they're like,' I said, 'they'll only worry.' Then, anxious to change the subject, I announced that Uncle Jack was coming for me at half-past nine to take me skating again. So we made our way back to the house.

When we turned into the yard we saw three men at the door talking to my grandfather. I thought they were probably Jehovah's Witnesses because I'd heard Aunt Hilda say that there were several in the area, going from door to door with their bibles and their leaflets. We noticed grandad shake his head and point towards the village. They nodded, thanked him and left. I asked him who they were and what they wanted.

'No idea, boy,' he said. 'They were asking after a family I've never heard of before.'

'Perhaps they were looking for the people who slept in the barn last night,' said Laura in a careless moment.

My mother, who was making some toast, asked nervously, 'What people?'

'Oh, it's nothing,' I said. 'Just Laura's silly imagination.'

My story-teller refilled our glasses. It was a good whisky and a perfect drink for the occasion, sipped leisurely throughout the long narrative which I did not want to end too soon. He paused to remember where he had left off:

Well, let's see. The rest of the day went as planned. By lunch-time I could skate reasonably well without using the chair. There were more people on the ice that morning and some of them were busy sweeping the snow from the courses where the speed races were to be held in the afternoon. Uncle Jack was disappointed that we couldn't stay for those because he wanted me to see what real fenland skating was like. Speed was the essence and the men bent over like reap-hooks to reduce wind resistance. They didn't go in for cutting fancy figures on the ice like some. Their aim was to travel as fast as they could. But we had to get back in time for Boxing Day dinner and so he put the chair into the car and opened the door for me. 'Another hour or two like that,' he said, 'and you'll have got the knack of it all right. P'raps if you come next year we'll be able to race each other.'

So Boxing Day came to an end and we walked home from Aunt Doris's back to 'Hollies End'. I began to feel that this Christmas had been so special that there would never be another quite like it, at least not at Common Acre. I think now I must have had an inkling of what my grandmother had felt.

There had been no more snow since morning and the night clouds were now transparent enough for us to see a few stars. I noticed that my grandfather was looking up at the sky too, but there was no sign of the comet. 'I don't suppose we shall ever know what that was all about, shall we boy!'

'What on earth are you talking about now?' grandma asked.

'Nothing,' he murmured. 'Nothing you'd understand.' Then he put his arm round my shoulders and gave me a hug.

There was a longer pause this time and eventually I had to ask how that special Christmas ended. Suddenly, he looked very tired.

We left 'Hollies End' the following morning soon after breakfast. Uncle Jack called for us and drove us back to Clayton. The Fens looked even bleaker than they had done on Christmas Eve. We turned on to a narrow road that ran parallel with the river before joining the main road. Some men were already out fishing and, further along the bank, two people were walking slowly towards the next village. The man had a large rucksack on his back and the woman was carrying a baby. Laura nudged me with her elbow but said nothing. I knew what she meant.

And I suppose you must think that's all rather fanciful. But, now that I live on my own I often think back to those days when, as a boy, I thought anything was possible.

We sat in silence for a few moments finishing our drinks. Then David Glassmoor slowly eased himself out of his armchair and limped over to the window, to look up at the sky. He was still standing there when I left.

2   *The Unknown Star*

There was a star which came from nowhere,
It shone one night in earth's dark sky.
Shepherds who knew each constellation
Looked up and asked the reason why.
Why was that strange light slowly moving
Over the hills, towards their town?
Brighter than flames or new made fire.
It held more awe than any crown.

They watched its journey, they gauged its height,
And were afraid at what they saw.
Its low flight stopped by the village inn,
Then poised above a stable door.
'What can it mean?' the shepherds wondered.
'Why has an unknown, glowing star
Stopped there above the broken roof-tops
Where our poor wintering cattle are?'

They came down swiftly from the hillside,
Down to the draughty, unlit shed,
To find a newborn child now sleeping,
A straw-filled manger for his bed.
Then kings from foreign countries travelled
Hour by hour, both night and day.
And the star, having served its purpose,
Ascended and drifted away.

3   Harps of Gold

There was a fire on the horizon. It glowed on the earth's hearth that was still wrapped in the shadows of a December night.

Some days the sun rises in a white heat that is blinding, as if it is but a fierce hole left in space by the last molten drop of creation, a monster's eye staring out of mythology.

But today it was blood-red, throbbing like a fresh wound that the clouds could not staunch. It inflamed the sky until its roundness was lost in a furnace of its own making.

'Red sky in the morning – shepherd's warning.' Is such a spectacular sunrise always a presage of bad weather to come? There is plenty of evidence to suggest that men have long believed so. St Matthew tells us that when the Pharisees and Sadducees asked Christ to show them a sign from heaven, He answered and said unto them:

> When it is evening, ye say, It will be fair weather,
> for the sky is red. And in the morning, it will be
> foul weather today for the sky is red and lowring.
> Oh ye hypocrites. Ye can discern the face of the sky
> but ye cannot discern the signs of the times …

Shakespeare, too was familiar with the proverb, which he quotes in *Venus and Adonis*:

> Like a red morn that ever yet betoken'd
> Wreck to the seaman, tempest to the field.
> Sorrow to shepherds, woe unto birds …

31

Alarming though such forebodings might be I was still excited by today's sunrise. It was a colourful beginning to Christmas Eve – which for me begins with daybreak, thereby helping to make one of the shortest days of the year as lengthy as I can.

And it is still possible in the Fens to hear the cockerel at break of day, even when the rest of the birds' dawn chorus is no more than a tentative appearance for the arrival of spring. Then there will be no more glorious sound for me than the skylarks in full song.

But today I have to be content with a cockerel and a garden robin who is waiting for the crumbs from my breakfast table. There he sits, red as a rear lamp glowing on the garden fence, cheeky as a boy caught trespassing, asking me to hurry up with my meal because he's hungry too. He is a regular visitor and a bit of a bully, resenting the wrens, blue tits, chaffinches and doves who daily use our bird-table as their 'take-away'. We also have spotted woodpeckers, tree-creepers, blackbirds and thrushes, but it is the robin who sits and out-stares me until I weaken.

Having fed the birds it is time to start putting the final touches to the decorations and I go out to cut some more greenery. The holly trees are so loaded with berries that we can still leave a generous display on the branches. The ivy, too, has an oily sheen that will prevent it from withering too soon in the house. Only the mistletoe is missing.

The Holly and the Ivy is one carol I would never want to lose from our repertoire. The words and the tune have a brightness that their annual repetition cannot dull and it is so quintessentially English:

> The holly and the ivy
> When they are both full grown,
> Of all the trees that are in the wood,
> The holly bears the crown
> *The rising of the sun*
> *And the running of the deer,*
> *The playing of the merry organ,*
> *Sweet singing in the choir.*

It evokes all those Christmasses imagined or recorded in fiction, poetry and art, yet the author of the words is unknown and presumably unaware of his popularity.

2

The red sky of the morning did not live up to its reputation, bringing neither trouble nor wreck to the shepherd or sailor.

As well as finishing the decorations there is the task of topping up the supply of logs outside the back door and then the delivering of presents to family and friends in the area.

By mid morning my wife and I are on our rounds, starting with those members of my family who still live in Whittlesey. It is a day that brings back many memories, especially of those Christmasses I spent with my parents.

Driving home along the north bank of the River Nene I noticed how high the water level was and that the nearby fields were, as usual, flooded and ready for skating, should there be a few days and nights of frost. The scene was not as arctic as it was some years ago when the river was frozen over, the ice thick enough for us to walk across, and the hungry swans came up to us to be fed.

Not many people have a picnic on the banks of the River Nene on Christmas Eve and I have to admit that ours was unpremeditated until we passed a fish-and-chip shop on our way out of the town. The smell was irresistible and we decided to be unconventional. Once the swans had tasted the hot chips they gathered eagerly round the car and demanded more. When we gave them some fish, our unexpected picnic became a shared feast and it was gratifying to know they'd also had something special for Christmas.

3

My day began with a fire on the horizon. It ended with a great crimson wheel disappearing slowly over the western rim of the world. Had there been any sound from that distance it would have been of a tolling bell fading into the shadows of the night.

It did not qualify as a fenland sunset because there were no clouds to reflect its dying light, not enough colour to quote the rest of the proverb – 'red sky at night, shepherd's delight'. The sun was now a closing eye that left the day to drift into evening.

And now it was truly Christmas Eve. Somewhere, in nearby villages, groups of carollers were again setting out on their last rounds. In towns noisier revelries were about to begin. A lighted inter-city 125 train slithered across the land, taking people home for Christmas.

It was time for us to return home too, to put a match to the fire, to draw the curtains, to put on a recording of carols, to pour a drink and prepare for our evening meal, which is always a special event for us and the highlight of the festivities.

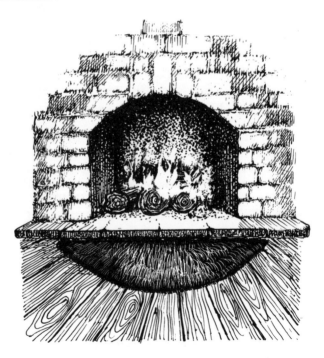

The singing began:

> It came upon a midnight clear,
> That glorious song of old.
> From angels bending near the earth
> To touch their harps of gold …

It couldn't fail. I looked at the Christmas tree, at the assortment of parcels soon to be opened, at the splendid display of cards we had received from our friends, and thought of the reason for it all. I still wanted to believe there was a reason. The story I had learned at the same time as I had learnt my nursery rhymes had not lost its power to persuade – at least not in the words of the Authorized Version of the New Testament. Some of the modern violations succeed only in persuading me how crass the translators are in debasing our language and in destroying a timeless narrative. Do we really gain anything by changing:

> And Joseph also went up from Galilee, out of the city
> of Nazareth, into Judaea, unto the city of David,
> which is called Bethlehem; (because he was of the
> house and lineage of David:) to be taxed with Mary
> his espoused wife, being great with child.
>   And so it was, that while they were there, the days
> were accomplished that she should be delivered. And
> she brought forth her first-born son, and wrapped
> him in swaddling clothes, and laid him in a manger;
> because there was no room for them in the inn …

To be reminded of those words and to hear the carols that have been written about that birth, is to know that the journey to the manger has to be in the heart as well as in the head.

> Still through the cloven skies they come,
> With peaceful wings unfurled;
> And still their heavenly music floats
> O'er all the weary world …

Too fanciful? Too unreal? Too easy to forget the truth of that night – the hunger, cold, rejection and anxiety of a family under suspicion? Only if we see the birth at Bethlehem as the end of the story rather than the beginning.

4   A North Bank Night Carol

Tonight the cold air magnifies the sky,
Loose nets of cloud are strung about the stars
And distant lights of cities rim the night
Bright as the late owl's frosty claws.

Tonight the sky has space about its ears,
A million years from sun to blazing sun,
And darkness feels as tangible as fire
That burns the face and scars the ungloved hand.

Tonight the grass and hedges sweat with ice,
The river locks the world behind its glass.
And that lone bird that swooped across the fields
Is caught by hungry winter and devoured.

Tonight inside a cold and windy barn,
Where cows and mice have eyes like holy flames,
A woman shapes the straw into a bed
And quietly bears the homeless Son of God.

5 Let's Keep the Nativity Play

Do you remember when the school Nativity play was as much a part of English life as Yorkshire pudding, Eccles cakes, or the Sunday school outing? It won't be for much longer, if we are not careful. Like many other customs that we take for granted it is under a growing threat from those reformers who think it is insensitive, if not offensive, to present in our schools a dramatized version of a story that every child will hear about, sooner or later, whether Christian or not.

The 6-year-old Josephs and innocent Marys may soon be things of the past, like silent movies or treadle sewing-machines. The Three Wise Men, the humble shepherds, the praising angels and a miracle birth, are now thought to be an insult to our intelligence as well as to our religious freedom. It is argued that the Nativity story is no longer relevant, acceptable, or necessary to a child's life or its education. The journey to Bethlehem is an antiquated fable that should be abandoned as a useless part of the imagination's discovery of wonder.

If that is so, we may as well get rid of all the Christmas trimmings, silver stars, shop window manger scenes, greeting cards and present giving, for they too are symbols of a belief that some old-fashioned survivors still wish to celebrate. And if we get rid of Christmas it follows naturally that we should also dispense with Easter. So let's get rid of hot-cross buns and Easter eggs. Somehow I do not think our modern temples of commerce – the great stores and shopping centres – would be very happy about such a prohibition.

Yet, some local authorities have already banned the display of any symbols that might remind us of those superstitious practices of a faith that now so easily offends. Despite the government's recent attempts to salvage that faith, especially in schools, there is an active opposition to the keeping of a tradition that surpasses religion. Guidelines are seldom enough to keep anything on track, as we have seen in other areas of our national life. It appears quite easy these days to throw out two thousand years of history, national or spiritual.

Of course people of other faiths, or no faith at all, have the right to think differently and I can also appreciate why some of us have become a little cynical when we see the confusing mess the Church has got itself into in the last few years. But to deprive young children of the joy of being in a Nativity play, for social or political reasons, is close to intolerance if not bigotry. In any case, shouldn't the children have a say in it too? From those I have talked to the answer is clearly yes.

The school Nativity play is surely more than a declaration of one faith. It is part of the season's celebrations, part of the wonderful, mixed-up pattern of tradition, make-believe and truth that life is all about. Threatened though it is, it can still pack school halls to the doors – and will continue to do so, I hope, for a long time.

If nothing else it is a play about birth, the problems, pains, joys and wonder of birth. It is a play about what happens when a new-born child is brought into the world, especially an unwanted one. It is also a play about giving and receiving, about light taking over from the dark, and about not judging a person because of his or her colour or lowly station in life. The achievement is always in the life lived.

But let me keep to one birth in particular. The shepherds and the wise men could not have expected to find this new child, about whom they had heard such wondrous things, simply wrapped in swaddling clothes, lying in a cow-shed, with only his tired, neglected parents looking on, wondering what next? The three kings must have imagined the birthplace to have at least the splendour of a palace. The shepherds must surely have thought that one of the rabbis in the town could have found a comfortable room in which this woman, whoever she was, could have had the child of which the angels had sung.

All these aspects come into it, of course, but we still miss the point of a children's Nativity play if we theologize about it too much, or find unacceptable social reasons for not wanting it to continue as a brief, annual part of school life.

I prefer to see it as an essentially legitimate play about innocence, a play in which children can dress up and be someone else in a story that happened once upon a time, the plot of which no one can really explain. They spend weeks learning their one or two lines and probably forget them on the night. The angel's halo might fall off, or a shepherd trip over his crook as he enters the stable, or the donkey might suddenly break in half and the baby doll be put in the manger the wrong way round. But it doesn't matter. It wasn't a very well organized birth anyway, not by today's standards. It was a rather makeshift affair in an unprepared place, with no midwife or hot water, at least according to St Luke. Had it been otherwise we would have lost the point of the story.

I have seen scores of Nativity plays and they have all been different. I have seen the traditional version of the New Testament simply dramatized and keeping faithful to the facts. I have seen modern versions which have tried to compete with popular rock musicals that have drawn on the scriptures for their story lines. And I have seen the impromptu productions where children, having learnt the bones of the plot, then flesh it out with their own spontaneous dialogue. This can have its unexpected moments of embarrassment for teachers and for parents. I can remember watching one infants' school presentation in which Mary was explaining to Joseph that she was expecting a baby. Joseph, knowing that it was nothing to do with him, shook his head reproachfully and said, 'Oh dear, Mary. Have you been a naughty girl again?' It brought the house down and no irreverence was meant. The child was simply growing up in a society where these things were openly talked about and either condoned, or condemned, without knowing the facts.

I have also seen black Marys and Chinese Josephs and, in one production, three little wise men from the east arriving on tricycles. One year the magi were heard to offer their gifts of 'gold, Frankenstein, and myrrh', which probably told us much about the choice of videos the children had been watching at home as it did about the scene of adoration in the stable.

A Nativity play for children must have an element of magic in it. Something happens that ought not to happen – like a miracle. There also has to be conflict between good and evil, between the angels and King Herod. In other words, it has to be a mixture of the traditional fairy story with a moral and the bible story itself. Every child has to have a part and be able to wear a costume. Why else would you want to be in a play, unless you can dress up?

A few years ago I was asked to write a Nativity play for 9 to 11-year-olds. I called it *The Miracle Tree* because the tree eventually had the power to grant the wishes of the children who came to it with genuine requests on behalf of others, rather than for themselves. I tried to present the doubts, temptations, disbeliefs and distorted values we can acquire if we cannot see the message of Christmas without understanding its real significance in the world today. And what is love about if it is not about giving and forgiving, gratitude and faith, joy and beginning again?

What I remember most about the play now is the colour, a stage full of bright characters and wide-eyed faces staring out into the audience, all hoping to spot their Mums and Dads who were unashamedly bursting with pride as the cameras recorded each scene for the family album. Some mothers could not resist joining the children in the singing of *Away in a Manger*, remembering perhaps when they were Mary or an angel, all of thirty-five years ago.

If there was a cynical tone in the opening paragraphs of this chapter, I trust it has now been dispelled by my obvious enthusiasm for the subject itself. I do not contradict what I said at the beginning. The Nativity play *is* threatened with extinction because Christmas itself is being challenged. We live in a world where we have to make room for a greater variety of faiths, attitudes and expectations, but I hope it will not mean that we shall also be guilty of not finding room for the true purpose of the festival which has brought joy to our winter months for many generations past.

When I asked some children recently what they would miss most if they no longer had Christmas I received, as one would expect, a very mixed reply. Some said they would miss all the presents and parties. Others placed more importance on the holiday from school and a visit to Florida or some ski resort. But one girl said, 'Please let's keep the Nativity play because I still want to be Mary before I'm too old.'

If nothing else it involves families in one of the greatest stories ever told and makes them pause for a few moments to ponder on what it is all about. Perhaps *its* guidelines are the ones we should follow if we are not to lose our way entirely.

6 Welcome to a Stranger

No longer under silent skies
    But at loud midnight He comes down,
To find each heart a Bethlehem,
    The doors still locked in every town.

He comes unnoticed through the dark,
    This quiet Stranger in the night.
We do not hear Him in the noise
    Or feel the radiance of His light.

He comes, and every house cries out
    'We have no room, no room, no room.'
Yet all He needs, He gently asks,
    Is our own being for His home.

He does not need the stable crib
    Or praising angels with bright wings,
He wants our eyes, our thoughts, our limbs,
    The use of ordinary things.

So open hearts and open house,
    Let Love find shelter where we are.
Kings cannot claim Him as their own
    Or riches buy that priceless star.

7 *The Man who Missed Christmas*

Sam Coates lived at the bottom of Adventurers' Drove for forty winters. There were few people in the area now who had known him as a young man but he was often talked about as one of the saddest men in the Fens.

His nearest neighbour was Hannah Goosetree who still lived in the pumping-station cottage a quarter of a mile away. The pumps had not been used since the 1947 floods when her husband Tom was the sluice-keeper. He had been allowed to stay on in the cottage, working for the river authorities as their resident mole catcher. When he died in 1974 his wife was given the right to continue as a tenant, paying a peppercorn rent for the privilege. The new electric pumps were operated by a central control, so lock-keepers and sluice-keepers were, like horse-keepers and blacksmiths, an almost forgotten breed.

Hannah always visited Sam Coates on Thursdays, taking him a batch of scones or a sponge sandwich that she had just baked. Although he kept both himself and his small wooden bungalow clean, he lived a very simple, frugal life. He had his pension and sometimes did a bit of casual work on the land when seasonal labour was needed, but he refused to take part in any social activities in the nearby village of Dexley and made it clear that he didn't want anyone to bother him, not even at Christmas.

It was Hannah herself who told me the story of how he came to be such a recluse and, at times, quite rude to those who tried to help:

Well, to begin with I think it's only fair to say that he

wasn't always like that. I can remember when he was
a young man working for Mr Harry Stackpole at
Nordyke Farm. He was his foreman then and a good
one too. He was not only an expert on the land but
a skilled mechanic as well. Must have saved his
master pounds. You could always tell a Stackpole
field round here 'cus Sam insisted on the best
ploughing he could get and he grew some of the best
crops in the Fens. He wouldn't let any of his men

plough a furrow with a dog's hind leg in it, I can tell you. It was the same at harvest. Everything had to be neat and tidy. He was married then, with two young children – a boy and a girl. His wife, Jenny, had a part-time job in the National Farmers' Union office in Morton, but I always found her a bit strange. Then tragedy struck. Their boy, Colin, was drowned in Martinmas Drain down by the south sluice. My Tom found him, poor little mite. He was only five years old. Jenny blamed herself for letting him out of her sight. She gave up her job and stayed at home, brooding. Everyone thought that she'd become very protective and possessive about their little girl, Linda. But it was just the opposite. She was always grumbling at the child and couldn't abide being on her own with her. Then the brooding soon became a sickness. She wouldn't eat, wouldn't go out. There were days when she wouldn't even speak to Sam. It took her all her time to get him a meal. He tried to make her see a doctor but she wouldn't hear of that either. He suggested that they went on holiday, but it was no good. She just got worse. Then one day, she disappeared – just walked off without a word of warning or explanation, and was never seen again. She left no note. Nothing. Sam called the police, of course, and there was a countrywide search for her, but she'd vanished. You wouldn't believe that anyone could disappear like that, would you? But she did. Left no trace. And, as far as I know, the mystery has never been solved and never will be now. There was even a rumour at the time that Sam had driven her to it, but that was a wicked thing to say about the man. I'd known him for a long time and I can tell you that he didn't know what had hit him. He was devastated. It soon became clear to his family that he wouldn't be able to bring Linda up on his own. During the summer months especially he was working up to fourteen hours a day and relied on his sister Ruth to look after the child for him. By the end of the year she decided there was only one sensible thing to do. Linda must go and live with her permanently. She and her husband had no children of their own, nor could they have. For the child's sake it would be better to make it more of an official adoption. Sam was reluctant to go that far but, in the end, he realized that his daughter needed a mother. So off she went. There were those who said he shouldn't have given in so easily, saying that he might get married again one day and want his child back. It does happen, I suppose. Anyway, Sam thought about it but stood by what he had done. You can't ring the bell backwards, can you! For a while he saw quite a bit of Linda, sometimes at the week-ends, occasionally during her school holidays, and also at Christmas. Then Ruth's husband got a job with a big food-processing firm in Essex and the visits became less frequent. Sam often confessed to me that he missed his little girl more than anything. I remember on one occasion he broke down and wept in front of me, then cursed himself for being such a weak fool. I told him he'd every right to cry, what with losing Colin, then Jenny, and now Linda. There's a limit to what anyone can take. And, as if that wasn't enough, he received a letter from his sister one day to say that they were emigrating to New Zealand, leaving that November and, naturally, taking Linda with them. That really broke him up. He tried to claim her back but the local authorities wouldn't hear of it. Linda was now seven and legally part of a family who, it must be said, loved her and would certainly give her a better chance in life. He went to see them off but from then on he was a changed man. He lost interest in his job and started drinking quite a bit. I never actually saw him drunk but he became very morose and moody. I don't think he cared whether he lived or not. He just wanted to forget. We tried several times to get him involved in the life of the village, or to take up a hobby, like golf or bowls. We invited him to come with us on our outings, or to share in our harvest suppers. But he'd have none of it. He wouldn't even spend Christmas with us and said he had no time for the Church and all that nonsense. After a while his boss, Harry Stackpole, asked him to move out of the foreman's house to the wooden bungalow in Adventurers' Drove, so that the bigger house could be given to a new work-hand with a large family. Sam resented it at the time but he didn't really have much choice. So that's where he lived, just him and his cat Charley. He even lost him in the end and if it hadn't been for my granddaughter Charlotte he might have died a much sadder man than he was. That's a story in itself, but I'm sure you've heard enough.

I urged Hannah to continue for I still wanted to know why the wooden bungalow was empty and what had happened to Sam.

Well, I don't suppose I shall ever forget that weekend. It was a week before Christmas and Charlotte had come to stay with me so that her parents could go on a shopping trip to London with some friends. They were going to stop overnight because they also wanted to see a show in the West End. I didn't mind. I loved having the child's company. She was eleven at the time and could talk the hind leg off a donkey or, on the other hand, she could amuse herself for hours. She was no trouble. I told her about Sam losing his cat and asked her to keep a look out for it. Mind you, I didn't hold out much hope. It could have been shot or poisoned, or killed on the road. As you know, they stray for miles and by the time a week had gone by I couldn't help thinking that Sam had seen the last of Charley as well. Anyway, we were sitting in the kitchen and, as usual, Charlotte was asking me all sorts of questions about Sam and why no one could do much for him. She'd have sat there all morning if I'd given way to her, so I suggested that she should go out and try to find me some ivy and mistletoe. 'There was plenty on

Mr Gale's oak tree last year,' I said, 'so I should look there.' Then the cheeky little madam said, 'What do you want mistletoe for? Are you hoping that someone's going to kiss you?' I had to smile. 'Just you remember, my girl, that I was as pretty as you once, if not prettier. Besides, it's not for me, it's for your mother.' She thought about that for a moment or two and then asked me what mistletoe had to do with Christmas. 'What have a lot of things got to do with Christmas?' I said. 'It's all part of our traditions, I suppose.' Then she wanted to know where all our traditions came from in the first place. So I then had to explain how most of them went back a long time, before Christmas was even thought of, and how people in those days used to believe that mistletoe helped them to find the person they would fall in love with one day and marry. It had magical powers. I suppose I should have said it was superstitious but that word didn't seem right somehow. I told her it was the same with Yule logs. 'The only Yule logs you'll ever see are those chocolate-covered rolls in the cake shops, but they don't really have anything to do with Christmas. That custom goes back thousands of years, to when people brought a whole tree trunk into their houses to burn through the winter. They believed that by keeping the wood burning they would also burn up all their hatreds and bad luck for another year.' I knew that I'd started something else then for my granddaughter is full of curiosity and loves hearing about unusual things. She folded her arms and leant on the table. 'Do you know any more stories about traditions?' she asked. 'I dare say I do,' I said, 'my mother and father were as full of stories as their parents had been and they always claimed that my grandmother had more stories in her head than a pillow had feathers.'

Hannah interrupted her recollections and said:

Well, you know how it was. We had nothing else

better to do in the winters those days. No television, no cars, no gallivanting off to London just when the fancy takes you. We had to make our own entertainment. I explained to Charlotte that at Christmas we used to play games like Snapdragon. And that was another mistake for she immediately wanted me to tell her what sort of game that was. 'Snapdragon,' I said, 'was an old game handed down from generation to generation and it wasn't a very sensible one when you stop to think about it. We'd get a large shallow bowl into which we put some raisins and sultanas, then we'd pour in some brandy and set light to it. The idea was to see if we were brave enough, or daft enough, to pick out the fruit while the flames were still burning. That caused some screaming and laughter my girl, I can tell you. Of course, the men could always do it easily with their thick skins, but the women were a bit scared. We preferred playing something like Postman's Knock or Black Magic because the winners then got the chance of dipping into the bran-tub to see what sort of prize they had won.' And you can imagine what her next question was. 'What is a bran-tub, gran?' So I had to tell her that it was a barrel – usually a grape or banana barrel from the grocer's, which we filled with sawdust. Into this we used to bury about twenty small parcels which were the prizes for the various games we played over Christmas. They were only small things because we'd had our main presents earlier in the day. It was up to luck what you pulled out. Sometimes our parents would put in some empty boxes just to tease us. 'Anyway,' I said to Charlotte, 'I thought you were supposed to be getting me some ivy and mistletoe. You'll get no lunch at this rate, so you'd better go now. And take Cromwell with you. He needs some exercise.' She loved taking my dog for a walk and often wished she could have one of her own, but her mother wouldn't agree to it. She claimed she was allergic to animals, which came as a surprise to me as she had grown up with them at home and I never saw anything wrong with her then. I think she just got too house-proud when she married. Her husband, Brian, is all right and we get on quite well with each other, but he has his own business and is very successful. He liked everything in the house to look just so! Anyway, off went Charlotte with the dog and I knew that she'd come to no harm in that part of the fen for there would be nobody about who we didn't know and couldn't trust. How much longer that will last I dread to think. You hear such dreadful things these days, don't you. Well, I suppose she had been gone for about an hour when back she came with a sheaf of ivy and a large spray of mistletoe under her arm. Then I noticed that she had something else in her hands. 'Where on earth did you find that?' I asked. She said she'd found it in Mr Gale's barn, lying abandoned in the straw. It was a little ginger kitten that still hadn't opened its eyes. 'And what do you propose to do with that?' I said. 'You know very well what your mother thinks about animals so you can't take it home, can you now. And I certainly don't want a kitten to look after.' I could see that she was disappointed. 'I thought perhaps we could give it to Mr Coates,' she said on the spur of the moment, 'you know, to make up for Charley.' I warned her that Sam probably wouldn't want the kitten either – Charley or no Charley. It was such a poor thing, anyway. 'But,' she said, 'surely we can go and see.' I knew Sam well enough to know that if he didn't want the thing he'd drown it as soon as our backs were turned, so I agreed that we might as well go down to the bungalow to see. It was some time before he answered the door and asked us in. I suppose it's easy for me to say that Charlotte is one of the loveliest, most appealing children you could ever wish to meet. She has such a gentle nature and her big brown eyes could coax a smile out of a statue. If she couldn't persuade Sam to consider taking the kitten then nobody would. But I was amazed beyond measure at what happened. Within minutes he became a different person, speaking to her as I'd never heard him speak to anyone else. It was as if something had suddenly come true for him, as if he had been waiting all these years for a child to visit him. There they sat, talking together like people who had known each other for a lifetime. I watched them – an old man and a young girl. His voice grew lighter. He smiled, he laughed. They talked about school, hobbies, animals, even Christmas. There was a brightness in the room that seemed to radiate from the hearthside where they sat. He held the kitten in his coarse hands and fussed over it. Then he turned to Charlotte and kissed her on the forehead. 'Thank you,' he said, 'thank you very much.' She looked at me with an air of innocent triumph. Had she spoken her mind at that moment I am sure she would have said, 'Nana, Mr Coates is not a rude and unfriendly man.' So that was that. When we got back to my house her parents were waiting, eager to tell us all about their exciting trip to London and the show they had been to see. I made them some coffee and then we told them what we had been doing. It was all a bit chaotic, as it always is when people are trying to impress. When all the talking was over they made it clear that they were ready to leave. 'Don't forget,' my daughter said, 'one of us will be over to collect you on Christmas morning.' Since my husband died I've mostly spent Christmas with my daughter. I have a son but he lives in Ripon and I'm not keen to go that far. Charlotte fetched her things from her room and gave me a kiss, without the mistletoe. I was always sorry to see her go because the house felt so empty without her. On this particular occasion it seemed even more noticeable. She's the only grandchild I see regularly. My son has two boys, nice lads, but they seldom come down more than twice a year. I think they find me a bit dull. (Hannah walked over to her china cabinet and took out a framed photograph which she showed me.) 'There they are. Handsome looking chaps, aren't they!' (She sat down again.)

Anyway, as I was saying, I was going to spend Christmas with my daughter and so the first thing I did that morning was walk my dog down to a friend who lived at the village end of the drove. She had two dogs of her own and was always prepared to look after Cromwell for me if I wanted a day out. It was a cold, grey day then, with a raw east wind that didn't bother to go round you. It made my eyes water and I pulled my scarf up to cover my ears. It was too cold for snow. You can imagine my surprise when I got back to my house to see Sam standing at the front door. He had two parcels in his hands. He offered me the first one which was wrapped in red paper and said 'That's for you, Hannah, for all the scones and sponge cakes you've made for me over the years. They were much appreciated. And this one's for the little 'un – I can't remember her name.' He squeezed my arm as he handed me a parcel wrapped in gold paper. 'Just wish her a merry Christmas from me and tell her that Charley's doing fine, just fine. I knew he'd come back some day.' Charlotte will be pleased, I said, and I wished him a merry Christmas too. But I have to admit, I was a bit worried about him. He looked in a kind of daze. I thought he might have been at the whisky bottle again but I couldn't smell it on his breath. 'Are you going to be all right?' I asked. 'I'll only be gone for a couple of days.' He smiled. 'Don't worry, old girl. I'm fine now.' And off he went, back to his bungalow. I gave Sam's present to Charlotte and she put it under the Christmas tree with all the others that were waiting to be opened. I couldn't help noticing later that it was one of the first she chose to open when the time came. I don't know where he'd got it from but it was a beautifully bound book of stories and poems. I just knew it would keep her happy for hours. It was only when I was looking through its pages in the afternoon that I noticed the date of publication. It was the same year that his daughter Linda had gone off to New Zealand with his sister Ruth. Had he bought it for her and, for some reason, been unable to give it her? Who knows. It was the same with the present he gave to me – a hand-carved jewellery box inlaid with mother-of-pearl. How long had he hoarded that? I know it makes me sound ungrateful, which I am not, but I still couldn't see Sam Coates going out shopping for Christmas presents. You know what they say, it's the thought that counts and a change had certainly come over Sam since Charlotte's visit. I thought about him all over Christmas and, as soon as I got back went down to see how he was. He appeared to be asleep in his chair. But I soon realized it was more than a sleep. His hands were colder than winter. His forehead like stone. I stood looking at him for several moments and noticed how his mouth had reposed itself into a smile. The fire was almost out but I could tell that it had been freshly lit that morning. An hour earlier, perhaps, and I might have been able to do something. That's something we'll never know. The kitten was still asleep in its basket near the hearth so I picked it up and took it home with me. Then I phoned the police and the ambulance. The rest all happened so quickly. I had no idea how on earth I was going to break the news to Charlotte, at least, not then. Naturally I went to the funeral. There was no church service for I knew Sam wouldn't have wanted one, and there was only a handful of mourners, mostly old people who had known him. We went straight to the crematorium. And that, I think, is really all there is to say. Harry Stackpole died some years back and his farms, and the bungalow, now belong to his son Nigel who lives near Ely.

I thanked Hannah for the story she had told me and left, my own curiosity almost satisfied. The black wooden bungalow was still there at the bottom of Adventurers' Drove, empty, boarded-up and now partly derelict. One more winter and it would probably be gone completely, with nothing left to be haunted – though it wouldn't surprise me to hear again one day that someone else had seen something unusual in that part of the fens.

One thing I do know now is that I had not imagined it.

8 A Ballad of the Nativity Cockerel

Some say the cockerel had never been known
To crow at daybreak until he knew
That Christ had been born in Bethlehem town.
So glad he was that he crew and crew –
Christus natus est.

He strutted about with his chest puffed out
And woke the hens in their nests of hay.
Get up! he crowed, with a confident shout,
And listen to what I have to say –
Christus natus est.

He walked from the barn and into the lane
To rouse the blackbird, robin and thrush.
Ring out, you sleepers, this joyous refrain.
Whistle these words from each bough and bush –
Christus natus est.

He leapt to the roof of the inn next door
Where they'd had no room or sheets to spare.
Awake! he cried, *no one's heard this before.*
Pay heed to the truth I now declare –
Christus natus est.

He went to the shepherds tending their sheep.
Arise! good folk from your weary night.
Down in the stable, no longer asleep.
A child is waiting to bring you light.
Christus natus est.

He flew to the palace where Herod raved
At three wise men who were on their way.
But he knew too well how the king behaved
And urged the Magi not to delay.
                    Christus natus est.

His crowing went out over land and sea
To all the cockerels that lived on earth.
You too have a gift and can sing like me
Each dawn with joy at our Saviour's birth –
                    Christus natus est.

He crowed so loudly and he crowed so long,
God told him to make the notes his own.
And from that moment his positive song
Became the one that we've always known –
                    Christus natus est.

9 Beneath the Water, Above the Land

St Agatha's Church looked as if it had been washed ashore during a storm and left there on the deserted mud-flats of the Wash. It was a squat building without spire or tower and had only a bellcote in which hung two unresonant bells.

Local people called it 'The Boat Church', not just because in times of mist it looked like a stranded boat, but also because its history was strangely connected with the sea and shipwrecks.

When the church was built in the late fourteenth century the North Sea came much further inland than it does today. But, with the gradual drainage of the Fens and the reclamation of land from the sea, the shoreline of the Wash was changed.

The parish of St Agatha at Gedney Far End was, for many of its incumbents, neither land nor sea but a small kingdom of its own fought over by wind and tide.

Eventually the tide won. After three hundred years of weathering the storms – sinking and tilting more as each year passed – the church was finally destroyed in the floods of 1763 and now there is no trace of it left.

Nor is there any sign of the houses that once made up its parish. Most of them succumbed even sooner, either to the weather or to pestilence and desertion. Families had been forced to leave the land after successive years of poor harvests. Plague and ague added insult to poverty. Villages were left derelict.

If, in its latter years, the church had any congregation at all it came from the neighbouring farms where stubborn marsh dwellers had survived, refusing to leave the land which they believed was now theirs by divine right.

More than one priest had pleaded with his bishop in Lincoln to be released from the living at Gedney Far End and, as these requests were usually accompanied by a crate of geese or a flask of smuggled brandy, the Lord Bishop was persuaded that the time had come for his clergyman to move.

But Father Bernard, who was to be the last vicar of St Agatha's, made no such demand. He liked a quiet life and saw it as his duty to stay there from the moment he was installed in 1746. Although his flock dwindled he was always willing to welcome those who wished to go to church and daily went through the offices whether anyone attended, or not. When some of his friends questioned the need for this he explained that he was there primarily to worship God and to pray for his people. Although the cold, damp building worsened his rheumatism, he enjoyed the solitary, candle-lit hour spent within its ancient walls.

The history of the church also meant something to him. There was, for instance, the story of how St Agatha came to be there in the first place. The legend claimed that in December 1326, a ship sailing from Holland to Whitby ran into a violent storm and was wrecked. The sixty passengers included four nuns who were being sent to establish a priory in Yorkshire. It was believed that all the passengers and crew were drowned. But, three days later, a small boat with two of the nuns was washed ashore at Gedney Far End. Both Sister Agatha and Sister Ursula were weak and near to death. Eventually their boat was seen by a wild-fowler waiting for the morning flight of geese to arrive on to the marsh. He went to get help and the two women were carried to the nearest house. Only Sister Agatha survived and she needed weeks of care from the village women before she was well enough to move. She stayed in the village until the spring, teaching the women new ways of baking, sewing and lace-making.

When their children were ill she nursed them back to health. Grateful for the way in which they had saved her life she vowed that one day a church would be built on the marsh as a permanent memorial to what they had done. Then she left and no more was heard of her until a bishop of Lincoln arrived many years later to consecrate the little church in her name. But, for the people of Gedney Far End, it was always referred to as the Boat Church.

Sister Agatha was not the last survivor of the sea's wrath to be washed up on those muddy shores of the Wash. In 1684 two sailors were found at low tide on the mud-banks and rescued by local fishermen. Then, in 1760, came the three men who rowed their boat as far as they could up the estuary, walked towards the church, where the candle-lit windows glowed warm in the winter dark and the metallic sound of the tolling bell ticked out like a clock.

Father Bernard had grown used to conducting the services to a diminishing congregation and an empty church. Had he been a younger man he might have sought a living somewhere else, but why regret? Now in poor health and crippled with his rheumatism, he was content to live out his days almost as a hermit.

His love for the church grew rather than waned. He polished the silver-plate, cleaned the floors, dusted the chairs, kept the candles burning and regularly laundered the altar-cloth. No one now came to evensong and only occasionally did he find two or three older people arriving on Sunday mornings for communion. His only constant companion was a blind dog called Samson that he had rescued six years ago from a trap on the marsh. Samson always sat in the choir stalls and followed the services.

Father Bernard observed the Church's calendar rigorously. Only a few of his ageing parishioners had braved the weather to attend services during Advent but he was determined to prepare for midnight mass on Christmas Eve with the same thoroughness as a priest expecting hundreds. He rang the service bell and lit the candles. He put on his best cope and processed towards the sanctuary. He said the general confession and pronounced the absolution, then began chanting the psalm for the twenty-fourth evening. His dog listened, ears pricked and twitching as the cold wind blew over the marsh. His master continued:

Open thou mine eyes, that I may see
the wondrous thing of Thy law.
I am a stranger upon earth; O hide
not Thy commandments from me …

Samson stirred, listened more intently and began to grumble with a deep, suppressed growl. Father Bernard was not disturbed and went on praying. Then he heard the click of the door latch and the door itself creak open. He finished the psalm, genuflected, and turned round. The three men stood at the end of the nave, their broad-brimmed hats in their hands, their faces unshaven and weary.

The priest beckoned to them and they approached the choir stalls where they then stood side by side, bewildered, even afraid. Father Bernard was sure from their manner that they had not come to harm him.

'Welcome!' he said. 'How glad I am that you have come.' He invited them to sit while he continued with the service. They did not speak, or take part, but watched and waited.

After their two days at sea in an open rowing-boat, the church felt safe and warm. The crippled priest would be easy to convince. He had probably been so long in this isolated place that he would know little of the affairs of the world, of wars, terror, famine and bloodshed that they had seen.

As they watched they began to think that the old man was already half out of his mind. Why else would he be conducting a service so late at night in an empty church, and talking to himself?

At last he turned to them and said in a loud joyful voice, '*Christ is born!*' Then he walked towards them and shook their hands as if they were long lost friends. 'What a tiring journey you must have had. I'm so glad you're here.'

The men looked at each other, trying to decide who should be the first to speak. At last one of them said, 'Is it really Christmas Eve?'

'Of course, my friends, why else would you be here?'

'But where are all the other people? Why is there no congregation?'

'Ah, that is a long story. But, first of all, why don't you tell me why you are here?'

They explained how they had been press-ganged into the Navy and shipped to France, how they had escaped as stowaways on one of His Majesty's ships bringing prisoners-of-war back to this country, how that ship had been blown off course and capsized in the North Sea, and how they had saved themselves by taking one of the small pilot-boats for their get-away. Now, to avoid being recaptured, they needed somewhere to hide and rest until it was safe for them to return to their families on Humberside. 'You see, Father, in this strong north wind, and with no stars to row by, we misread the coastline and are not sure where we are.'

Father Bernard took some time to consider their statement. But the men, not aware of what he was thinking, pressed their claim. 'We need only a few days and then we'll be gone … There'll be no trouble … just a place to sleep, some food … someone we can trust.'

The priest did not need reminding that it was on such a night that Mary and Joseph arrived in Bethlehem and were unable to find a room in which their child could be born. He also knew that he would be able to offer them something better than a stable. 'You must come with me,' he said. 'I live alone now with my dog and my house would not be to everyone's taste. It is simple, as is my food. But you are welcome. The one thing I do have is some good ale.'

He blew out the candles and led the men out of the church, along the track leading to the vicarage. If they wanted to kill him, now was the ideal moment. No one spoke until they reached the house.

Soon they were all sitting before a blazing log fire, their tankards of ale warming on the hearth. They sat and talked on until day broke, at which point Father Bernard rose to greet the Christmas morn by opening the shutters and offering up an impromptu prayer of thanksgiving.

He turned and smiled at his guests. 'Do you know, this is the first time in many years that I have been able to entertain friends for Christmas in my own home.'

'Are you not worried, Father,' asked one of the men, 'that we shall be found, with you as our accomplice?'

The priest chuckled. 'It's unlikely out here. Besides, we must trust. Without trust we know nothing but fear.'

The three strangers stayed with Father Bernard for two days, resting, eating, drinking and talking about their ordeal until they felt they had to move before his house was completely bare.

With Father Bernard's help and knowledge of the area they planned which route they would take as far as Grimsby. He gave them food for the journey and wished them God's speed.

As the men shook hands with him they said, 'We will repay you, Father, as soon as we can. Your cupboards will be full before summer and your barrels replenished.'

When they had gone Father Bernard sat alone wishing that he could have had their company for a little longer. He was still not sure who they really were but if he had been able to help them in some way, he was satisfied. He gently patted his dog's head. 'We never know, do we Sam, who we entertain in our home, or who we turn away.'

A few months later a travelling carrier arrived at the vicarage with three parcels and a barrel of ale. Had Father Bernard been there to open them he would have found in one a selection of cheeses, in the second a box of dried fruits, and in the third a model of his church carved out of bone. But his house was now empty. The old priest had been taken ill early in the New Year and was moved to the hospice at Heckington to be cared for by the Sisters of Mercy. No more services were held at St Agatha's. Already some of the windows were broken and the small churchyard overgrown with nettles. The only people who lived near the vicarage were two bachelor brothers who still farmed a few acres and went fishing. When the carrier found out from them what had happened to Father Bernard he knew there was only one thing to do, take his deliveries to the hospice on his way home.

Although the priest was still alive he was too weak to appreciate the gifts that had been sent to him by the men he had helped. He died in early April and during the following summer a memorial was erected in the churchyard at Gedney Far End. It would have stood there for years had the storms of 1763 not destroyed all that was left of the church and the village. For several days high tides and gale-force winds had plundered the east coast. Sea-walls collapsed and the whole of the Lincolnshire marshland was submerged. The windows of the church cracked and fell in; the stones crumbled and the building slowly sank, like a wrecked boat into the mud.

For some years afterwards visiting wild-fowlers claimed that they occasionally heard the tolling of a bell at low tide and, when the land was eventually reclaimed, farmers told of how they sometimes ploughed up stones where stones were not expected.

But the spirit of St Agatha went beyond the waters and the land. So did that of Father Bernard. To walk along that sea-wall now, especially at Christmastime, is to feel a presence greater than nature can generate or explain.

10 The Letter
that Came at Christmas

Although Mrs Whitmore was looking forward to spending Christmas again with her daughter and family, she also knew that there would still be moments of sadness, as there always had been for that last seventy years or more. The fact that she was approaching her ninety-third birthday did not in any way diminish her memory and she never let a year pass without reminding her grandchildren and great grandchildren that her husband had been killed on the Somme battlefields in December 1916 when he was only twenty-one.

We'd only been married eighteen months. I was then nineteen and Frank was two years older. The last time I saw him was soon after I'd had my first child – the only one as it happened. Janet always wanted a sister when she was little, but I told her they didn't grow on trees and I had no intention of getting married again.

Frank came home on leave for seven days before being sent to France. I shall always remember it. It was the last week in August 1916. It wasn't a particularly good summer but those few days were heaven. The sun shone and we went for walks in the country, pushing our baby in the pram. 'You will come back to me, won't you?' I kept saying. 'You will come back!' I must have said it a hundred times. He always assured me that he would but I knew in his heart that he was afraid. He'd heard from some of the lads who were sent home wounded what it was like out there. He wasn't looking forward to going. He was no hero. His great dream was to have his own little shop. He'd worked for Ransons the grocer's ever since leaving school. 'One day,' he used to say, 'we'll have our own business. People'll allus want food and there'll allus be people.'

I never knew any other boy but Frank. We started going out with each other as soon as our parents gave their consent. Our families had lived in the same town for years. There wasn't much we didn't know about each other in a small place like that. But you still had to get your parents' approval to start courting, not like today. Frank had three brothers who were all younger and they used to tease us for being so serious. Two of them were later lost in the war. They never did find Jack's body. He was only seventeen.

We were too young to get married, of course, but people did then. The war had already started and I suppose everybody felt a kind of urgency about things. Everything had to be done in a hurry. Frank didn't volunteer immediately because he believed, like a lot of others, that it would be over quite quickly. But they were all wrong. Far from getting better, it got worse. The whole world seemed to be turned upside-down by that war. It wasn't always patriotism that made them go either. Young men who held back were given a rough time, especially by certain well-off young ladies who thought every man should be in uniform. Frank took a lot of abuse in the shop and decided, as much for my sake as his, to join up before he was called up. That was in the January. He was sent to France in September and killed on December 4th. I received a letter from his commanding officer just two days before Christmas Day. And that was it. There was no carol singing with the Germans for him. I just couldn't believe it. I suppose the time came when I had to accept that he wasn't coming home but I can't remember when it was. The War Graves Commission later sent me a photograph and plot number to show where he was buried, but I thought what good is that? I don't suppose I shall ever have the chance of going out there to visit him.

It's surprising what you miss. Not only Christmasses, but birthdays and anniversaries. I just had to manage the best I could. Eventually I got a War Widow's Pension of eighteen shillings a week. Then, when Ransons closed down, I ran a little grocery shop from our front room. We lived in a two-up, two-down terrace at the time for six shillings a week. Then the landlord built a wash-house on the back and put the rent up another shilling, so there wasn't much left for luxuries. A lot has happened since then, hasn't it! People say they can't live on eighty pounds a week now. That's more than we had for a whole year.

I did eventually go out to see where Frank was buried but it was not until 1968 for the fiftieth anniversary of the signing of the Armistice. I'd always said I'd never go. There were times when I thought he'd just come walking down the street, like he used to, whistling on his way home from work. Then the Second World War came and another generation was slaughtered.

I knew some women who had been out to the cemeteries and, in the end, they persuaded me to go on their trip which had been organized by the British Legion. There were about forty of us – war widows, relatives, even two of the old soldiers who had survived the trenches. I couldn't believe I was still living in the real world as I sat in the ferry lounge sipping a glass of sweet sherry. I looked through the window at the great expanse of grey sea which surrounded us and thought, this is the same stretch of water that Frank must have seen all those years ago. Not the same waves but the same sea that took him from me, and I resented it.

It was the first time for me to leave the country and

I was very nervous. They took us everywhere by coach – Ypres, Vimy Ridge, Passchendaele, Tyne Cot and the Somme. It was very well organized, very moving. I'd always imagined it to be just like the pictures, all mud, barbed-wire and craters. But it was green, with lots of flowers and well-kept paths. There were parties of schoolchildren there, too, taking photographs of each other and laughing. Was this where it all happened, I kept saying to myself? Then, at Thiepval, I came face to face with the reality of it all. We walked slowly through the great arched monument with its 72,000 names of the missing dead with no graves, and down the steps to the cemetery with its regimented rows of white headstones. Somewhere among them was Frank. I looked at the piece of paper with its reference number, which I had unwittingly crumpled in my hand. The grass between the rows was still wet from earlier rain, the rose-bushes in flower. It was so peaceful. The only people near me then were two gardeners quietly forking over the soil round the stones. I just had to pause before each grave. It was like carrying out an inspection. The stones stood clean and erect, as if the men were still on parade. In some ways it was a bit like visiting a hospital of ghosts. But the beds were empty. Then, there it was, after all that time. The moment I had tried to delay, the name I had come to see – *Private Frank Whitmore – Aged Twenty-one – Killed in Action – December 1916.* A small, stark stone with his regimental emblem and a simple cross carved by an unknown hand. It was as if all the years had rolled away and our brief life together had been restored for that one moment. I felt my heart pounding and a lump rise in my throat. It was like falling in love all over again. Can you understand what I mean? Frank had not grown old. He was still twenty-one and would soon be coming home. And then I realized how old I was, with a grown-up daughter and grandchildren. Of course Frank wouldn't be coming home. There would be no more Christmasses

together, no more birthdays or anniversaries. I put the piece of paper into my handbag and rejoined the rest of the party.

To end the tour we were taken back to Ypres for our last night and, at eight o'clock, we stood at the Menin Gate for the ceremony of sounding The Last Post. Even the men couldn't keep back their tears any longer as those haunting notes broke the silence of the air.

Mabel Whitmore remained silent too for a few seconds and I thought that she had probably told me all she wanted me to know. I felt that in half an hour I had shared most of her life. Soon she would be getting ready to spend another Christmas with her daughter and family. She didn't look ninety-three. Her hair was still quite thick and her cheeks were soft and smooth. Only her hands seemed to give her age away. They were clenched and wizened, as if they had never relaxed since that Christmas of 1916. Then she stood up and went over to her bureau drawer.

From it she took out a bundle of letters, most of them still in their brown envelopes. 'Would you like to have a look at some of these?' she asked. 'They're Frank's letters. Be careful how you handle them. They're very fragile now.'

I took them gently from her. It was as if she had given me a wounded bird to hold. I smelt the yellowing pages but knew that I could never bring myself to read them. They were a young man's love-letters, from another time, another world. I doubted if they could tell me anything more than I already knew of that awful war. I didn't want to pry.

After a few moments I handed them back to her. 'Thank you,' I said. 'They must be very precious to you after all these years.' Words are always difficult on such occasions. 'Perhaps you should imagine that they have just arrived,' I said.

'I often do,' she replied.

There was a ring at the front door. 'Ah! That will be the postman now,' she said eagerly. And, like a young woman, she hurried out of the room.

11   *Another Season, Another Time*

The weather was cold enough for Christmas. A north-easterly wind blew over the washlands near Whittlesey and there was rain in the air. It was late May.

I was on my way to a reunion between two German ex-prisoners-of-war and two former land-army girls who had agreed to share with me some of their memories of what Christmas was like for them at the end of the Second World War.

It was appropriate that the house to which I had been invited was in the street where I had spent my childhood and where, in 1945, I had wildly celebrated that still uncertain victory in Europe.

The street then was dressed with bunting, Union Jacks, coloured lights, portraits of Winston Churchill and the Royal Family, and home-made banners proclaiming peace. The bells of St Andrew's Church rang out for the first time in five years and tired neighbours were seen dancing. Trestle-tables were erected in the middle of the street for the children's parties and there was a lot of noise.

It all seemed a very long time ago, as if I had lived on earth before and was now revisiting history. Several of those old houses had been demolished after the war and many of the people I knew have died. Such a street inevitably exudes its own air of sadness and I was not surprised to see a funeral cortège slowly making its way to the church.

What with that, and the weather, the day could not have started more depressingly, so I was grateful to see a lively fire burning in the room where I was to eavesdrop on the recollections of what life was like for other people in those years when that calamitous war came to an end.

I had already met Betty and Ernie Spridgeon on a few, brief occasions but Hans, Eric and Heather were strangers and I was not at all sure how much they would be prepared to tell me.

Hans and Eric had both been prisoners at the Thorney POW camp but had not seen each other since. Betty and Heather were Land Army Girls together in the same village and had kept in touch over the years. With so many memories to recall, and with each person wanting to add to whatever was being said, I need not have worried about a shortage of detail or humour.

I had been given some background information about the prison camp by my friend, Hugh Cave, who, in 1945, was instructed by the Ministry of Works to oversee and construct, as quickly as possible, the campsite at Park Farm, Thorney.

The camp was intended to accommodate up to a thousand prisoners who were being transferred from Sheffield, Bolton, Bury and Manchester. Additional labour was provided by a hundred German prisoners who were already at Friday Bridge, near Wisbech.

Initially the camp was made up of large tents with a coal-house and ablution block constructed of asbestos and timber. Eventually all the tents were replaced by Nissen huts, complete with electricity.

Hans Neibels was among some of the earliest arrivals in 1945, having been transferred from an overcrowded camp in Lancashire. He was called up on 12 June 1944 and captured on 21 September of that year. 'I was Adolf's last hope,' he said, 'and had no choice in the matter.'

Eric Koehler was only just over sixteen when he was captured on the Belgian border. He arrived at the Thorney camp in December 1945. 'And I can remember it was bloody cold in the tents that winter,' he said, adding, 'forgive my bad language but the first English words I learnt were swear words.'

Both men agreed that to use the word 'imprisonment'

was not an entirely accurate description of their conditions, certainly not when compared with some of the more notorious prison-camps in Germany.

'There was a minimum of barbed-wire round the camp,' said Hans, 'just one strand, that's all.'

Eric nodded in agreement. 'We were even told to guard ourselves some times. But, mind you, we were not allowed to forget who and what we were.'

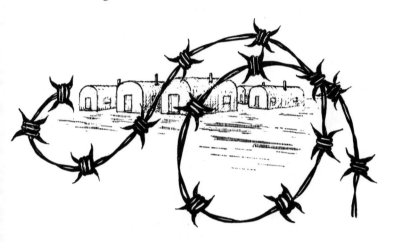

I asked them if they had ever tried to escape. Hans said, 'What was the point? There was nowhere to go unless we could get to Ireland and hope for repatriation from there.'

Eric admitted that he had tried once but realized that if he got away there would probably be little to go home to in Germany. Before his call-up he had seen something of the sustained bombing-raids by the Allied Air Forces. 'They left nothing standing. Street after street was demolished until the town was a heap of rubble. I suppose in the end I decided that life was going to be better in the camp.'

'And the prisoners got more food than us poor civilians,' said Betty who'd lived in the Land Army hostel close by. 'In winter they often had fires and plenty of hot water when we didn't.'

All these comments could now be made in a spirit of

friendship for both Hans and Eric had married English girls and had chosen to make Britain their home and adopted country. Heather, Eric's wife, had lived in the same hostel as Betty and could remember how they used to queue up for a bath after a hard day's work. 'We were paid twenty-eight shillings a week then. It was back-breaking, too.'

'You were lucky,' said Eric. 'We were given one shilling a day and could only spend that on the camp.'

With mock indignation Betty said, 'But you were prisoners. We weren't – at least I don't think we were.'

In the early months at the camp any fraternization between the Germans and British girls was strictly forbidden but, as most of the prisoners were taken out to work on the neighbouring farms where the land-army girls were also employed, it was a difficult regulation to enforce.

'Could we really be expected to work with someone all day without speaking to them?' said Betty. 'I couldn't. It wasn't human.'

'It didn't last long though, did it?' said Heather with a chuckle. 'D'you remember there used to be an empty hut at the back of the camp where some of 'em used to do their courting, or whatever. There was a helluva row when the commanding officer found out about that.'

The 'courting' not only continued but also succeeded because quite a few of the prisoners married local girls and settled in this country to become, like Eric and Hans, naturalized British subjects. Eric admitted that he now felt as English as anybody else and even found it difficult to converse now in German. He loves reading English books, walking the English countryside, and living in the small fenland village of Wicken, where I can recall hearing some good stories in The Maid's Head more than twenty years ago.

I asked him what he could remember most clearly about those early years when he was a young prisoner-of-war – and kept as one until the end of 1947, as most of his countrymen were.

'I can certainly remember that first Christmas of 1945

very well. I worked on Christmas Day, pulling up sugar-beet when there was five inches of snow on the ground. We had to dig through the snow with our bare hands, pull up the beet, knock them together, and then pile them into heaps. It was hard work I can tell you. I was still a boy, in a way, trying to make sense of it all.'

'Did you volunteer to go into the Army?' I asked.

'No one volunteered in Germany. If you did not go into Hitler's Youth Army you were conscripted and had to take your chance. I was captured near Arnhem and saw enough of the terrible things that war can do to people. There were atrocities on both sides. So, pulling sugar-beet was better than killing people. And, I must say, our troops were told – if you are going to get captured, get captured by the British!'

'All the same,' I said, 'it doesn't sound as if you had much of a Christmas celebration that year.'

Hans explained that they had never celebrated Christmas in the way that we do. 'You English must have big parties, lots of drink and presents. In Germany, when I was young, it was more of a religious time. We thought the most important thing to do on Christmas Eve was to go to midnight mass.'

'So you didn't decorate your huts at the camp, or have a Christmas tree and a sing-song?' I asked.

'No. We sometimes sang a carol and thought of our families. But on Christmas Day the cattle had to be fed, the cows milked, and what does Christmas mean away from home anyway!'

'One year we did make some whisky,' said Eric. 'It was very good too. Very strong. We made it from sugar-beet, potatoes, wheat and yeast. We distilled it from an old kettle.' His mischievous eyes sparkled at the thought of it. 'And the farmer we worked for sometimes gave us a packet of cigarettes.'

'Yes, we were lucky being here in the Fens,' said Hans. 'The farmers knew that they had got some good workmen and that we didn't waste time, so they'd often give us something extra to show their appreciation. The one thing I learnt about fen-people is that they like value for money.'

What I had also learnt from Hugh Cave was that the camp at Thorney had a very good male voice choir and theatrical company. Indeed, the more the camp became established, the more it became a world unto itself. The prisoners built their own theatre, workshops, recreation rooms and shops. They organized football teams, lecture courses, an orchestra – 'anything,' said Eric, 'to keep our brains busy.'

The camp also became an accepted part of village life. The daily event of the prisoners being taken off in lorries to work on the farms caused no more raised eyebrows than the local children going off to school.

'One of my most vivid memories of those years,' said Hugh, 'is of the first concert given by the prisoners who had formed themselves into a choir. This was before they had built their theatre and so they gave the concert under the trees, to an audience of VIP's. The sound was wonderful.'

By the end of 1945 there were more than fifty Nissen huts, separated by concrete paths and flower-beds. The camp was now truly a village within a village, with several of the prisoners setting themselves up as the tradesmen they had been before the war – cobblers, carpenters, tailors, barbers and gardeners. Some were also motor mechanics and established their own garage where they serviced and repaired the camp's military vehicles, presumably saving the British taxpayer a little money.

Hugh explained to me how his men had helped to build the theatre:

We had been able to salvage a lot of material from an American Army dump near Whittlesey. It was surprising what they had left behind. The theatre had a proper auditorium with a sloping floor, with the rows of seating made up from an assortment of settees, armchairs and car seats. There was also an orchestra pit, stage-lighting, and a high roof with 'flies' into which they could winch up the scenery. It wasn't long before they were able to put on some very professional shows because they also had some excellent musicians and actors.

Betty Spridgeon confirmed this was so for she has dozens of photographs and copies of programmes for the shows that the prisoners did produce. Album after album came down from off her shelves as names were recalled and it was fascinating to watch Eric and Hans trying to remember some of their comrades of fifty years ago.

As we looked through her scrap-books of letters, press-cuttings and photographs I watched these two ex-prisoners reliving many of those occasions, remembering the words of most of the songs, the sketches and characters of another time. I also noticed that in some of the photographs of the cast there appeared to be some very voluptuous blondes. Were they by any chance the land-army girls? No, they were some of the prisoners in drag, complete with shapely bosoms, make-up, long dresses, high heels and stockings, looking as glamorous as any film star.

Music was clearly an important feature of camp life and, in having the gifted Alois Prigo as one of their fellow prisoners, they had a professional composer, arranger, pianist and musical director in residence. 'We even made some of our instruments,' said Eric. That was not all. They also made puppets and lots of wooden toys for the local children; they made slippers out of balls of string for the land-army girls, and they made an altar-cloth for Thorney Abbey – which was later stolen. One special toy was a large doll's house which was presented to the camp commandant – Major Hobbs. This eventually found its way to Australia.

In 1946 the village schoolmaster gave permission for his school gymnasium to be used for a public production of an operetta, *Geschwister – Brothers and Sisters*, which was written and composed by another talented prisoner, Hans Laube, who came from Thuringen. Those prisoners who were not involved in the large cast were active behind the scenes. The audiences were enthralled. As with all the camp's musical activities it was a great success because the men had plenty of time for rehearsals and their performances were always of a high standard.

The following Christmas the choir was invited to sing in Peterborough Cathedral and I have recently spoken to people who can remember it as a thrilling and moving experience, especially when the choir sang *Stille Nacht, Heilige Nacht*.

Eventually the running of the camp passed from the British Military to the War Agricultural Committee – a move that was not popular with the German prisoners. 'It was more like living under the Gestapo,' said Eric. 'We got on well with the British officers, who were always very fair, but the civilians were real …' He hesitated. 'Well, you know what I mean – B.S.B's!'

'I was lucky,' said Hans. 'I was billetted out to a farmer at Turves, near Coates, and he treated me like I was his son. We got on very well together and he even gave me the key to the house so I could let myself in late at night.'

Eric spent some of his time in captivity at other camps, particularly in Norfolk and on the borders of the Fens. He can remember the disaster of the 1947 floods when the whole of the fen country was threatened with inundation. He was working on a bulldozer at Southery. Hundreds of prisoners took part in that campaign, sand-bagging, strengthening the dykes, trying to prevent more river-banks from bursting, evacuating animals. But it was mostly a lost battle. 'One day the king came to see the work for himself and he said to one of the officers in charge, "Why are all those men wearing yellow patches on their backs?" The officer replied, "Well, your Majesty, they're prisoners!" And do you know, I don't think the king could understand why we were still wearing prison uniform.'

I then asked both men how they had celebrated our VE Day. The simple answer was that they had not. They were afraid to appear too jubilant because they knew that among the prisoners at that time were men who were still loyal to the SS and would report them for treason if they ever got back to Germany. 'You won't believe this,' said Hans, 'but they still believed that all the talk about the Allied victory was propaganda. They had been so brainwashed into believing that Germany could not be beaten that if we had celebrated your victory they would probably have lynched us. They soon found out, of course, but you couldn't trust them. I certainly hope that we never see their like again.'

More photographs, more letters, more reminders of the men who were forced to spend their Christmas away from home, as many of our countrymen did. There were the inevitable moments of sadness as they talked about comrades who had since died, either in this country or in the post-war Germany to which they had returned. 'It all seems such a long time ago now,' said Eric. 'We were only boys.'

Betty and Heather were now involved in their own memories of their land-army days. Because Betty is such a tenacious tracker-down of people from the past she has been able to trace all but two of the girls who were based at Thorney. They have had many reunions and have been featured on television and radio programmes. 'And, do you know what we each received as a reward for our war efforts?' asked Betty. 'Not a medal or a gratuity. We were given our uniforms, which were already nearly worn out, and our boots. But still, we mustn't grumble, we did form some wonderful friendships which have lasted much longer.'

Betty's husband, Ernie, who served in the Royal Navy during the war and then as a lorry-driver responsible for getting the prisoners or the land-army girls to their farms, must have sat through many hours of reminiscing and probably knew as much as anyone there. 'We could always get you a few more ex POW's to talk to,' he said, 'if this morning has not been what you expected.'

I assured him it was just what I wanted and that the morning's interview could have gone on for another three hours. Had it done so I could only speculate on how many more pots of tea and cups of coffee he would have made in that time.

As it was, I had to leave at twelve-thirty for another nostalgic engagement, allowing them all to go on reliving their pasts without my asking them too many questions.

The funeral had left the church. The street where I had once been an onlooker on the fringe of those war-time years, now felt even more strange and empty.

As I drove back over the washlands I was grateful that the May weather had deteriorated even more into Decemberish gloom for it helped me to imagine those winters of fifty years ago when grey was a predominant colour and our peace still very uncertain. The war had changed too many things.

But that was then. Now, as this morning proved, life is very different and the festivities of Christmas have never been more extravagant. Not for the right reasons, perhaps, but I doubt if the people with whom I spent such a delightful time would want to go back to an age when the season was forced to be less than one of goodwill and rejoicing.

12 Beyond His Birth

When the child lay in the manger
Was there a woman in the night
Who felt the shock-waves of his birth
Her life of darkness seared with light?

Was there a lame man in the square
Who thought his legs twitched then to feel
A hand reach out and touch the limbs
He had been told no one could heal?

Was there a woman in the crowd
Who felt her crippled hands unfold
When she but plucked those swaddling clothes
And saw his smile pierce through the cold?

Was there a blind man in some street
For whom closed eyelids were unlocked
Because within a stable slept
A child who in love's cradle rocked?

Did Lazarus feel before his time
A second life beyond his death,
And dying children dance again
Because from somewhere came new breath?

Did fishermen feel the slack tide turn,
A calm wind tame their troubled sea?
And what of the hungry multitudes
Gathered beneath each olive tree?

None knew it then but all that night
Were touched by One whose birth, we know,
Changed the direction of the stars
And half the destinies of earth below.

13   The Two Brothers

Our town always had its share of characters – barmy,
recalcitrant, eccentric, rebellious and quaint. Most were
harmless if left alone. There was crazy Phyllis who went
cartwheeling down the street, revealing to all who cared to
look that she was again knickerless. Then there was Willy
Oxo who worked as a handyman on the Friday market
and at auction sales. He lived in a caravan near the
cemetery and earned his nickname 'Oxo' because he was
always boasting that he kept his savings in an Oxo tin in
the bottom of a chest of drawers behind the door.
'Nobody'll find it there,' he'd say, in a loud confident
voice.

   If I allowed myself time to stop and think about them all
I could fill pages with their escapades and sayings. There
was Sandy Bridegroom, a bachelor who kept his goats in
the churchyard and played the bass drum in the local
town band. He couldn't read or write but had a strong arm
and loved marches. He often took his drum with him into
the churchyard to 'get in a bit of practice where it's nice
and quiet' and those already buried there must have
thought more than once that the dawn of resurrection day
had come. Sandy acquired his nickname because he had a
reputation for appearing at everybody's wedding and
claiming that the bride had jilted him. He was a short,
stocky little man with red hair and when the drum was
strapped to his chest he couldn't see over it, which was a
problem when it came to parades. On those occasions he
had to be told which route the band was taking and follow
the sound. That worked fairly well until one Sunday

when, for a special British Legion parade, the march through the town was re-routed. For some reason this information did not reach Sandy. Consequently the band went one way and he another. To his dying day he maintained that he had got it right and everybody else was wrong. 'I was,' he would say, 'the only one to finish properly.'

This story, however, is not about Sandy or any of the other individuals I have mentioned, but about two brothers who were also bachelors and ran a kind of rag-and-bone business. Their names were Barney Stickle and Freddie Stickle. Neither had ever looked young and neither seemed to grow any older with the years. They were caught like a couple of hairy spiders in a time-warp, aged forever sixty.

Their backyard also had an air of timelessness about it, as if history had dumped in it all the outdated, unwanted, paraphernalia of the town – broken prams, push-chairs, iron bedsteads, rusting mangles, milk churns, armchairs, gin-traps, sickles, scythes, zinc baths and bottles – hundreds of bottles, including, no doubt, a few Lady Hamiltons.

Barney, who was five years older than Freddie, saw himself as the master and often treated his brother more like a backward son. Both were inclined to be 'three bricks short of a load' as we say in this part of the Fens, but Freddie was sometimes intimidated to a degree of imbecility that made him worse than he probably was. In his simple rough way he was a sensitive person and was quickly moved to tears.

As their business did not bring in much money both had part-time jobs. Barney was a chimney-sweep and Freddie a milkman with a word for everyone. Even if it was pouring with rain he would call out, 'It's a nice day, so far!' And whenever he saw a young mother he would shout across the street, 'Have you fed the baby, missis?' Then he would push his trades-bike a few houses along, calling 'Milko! Freddie's here!'

Barney was the opposite – taciturn, suspicious and unfriendly. The children of the town were afraid of him and did not like being sent to the scrap-yard to sell something their parents no longer needed. Nor did they stay near their own houses when Barney came to sweep the chimneys. He had threatened to push more than one child up into that 'everlasting darkness' if they didn't keep out of his way. 'In the good old days,' he'd say, 'they used to send little beggars like you up the chimneys to eat the soot.'

Just as their nature and part-time jobs were so very different, so too were their beliefs – political and religious. Barney was a staunch Tory and Freddie a Socialist. On election days they each wore the appropriate coloured rosettes of their respective parties and didn't speak to each other until the following day. Similarly, when it came to religion, Barney was an agnostic and Freddie a Christian. This became a particular source of friction at Christmas time. Barney wanted nothing to do with it and would have abolished the festival altogether if he could. Freddie loved it as a child. He liked to decorate the house with paper-chains, listen to carols on his little battery wireless set and, for all we know, still believed in Santa Claus.

When it came to belonging to a place of worship, it would be true to say that Freddie was a worshipper of no fixed address. Sometimes he was a Methodist, sometimes a Baptist, and then for weeks he would go to the Salvation Army so that he could wear a uniform. He liked his uniform so much that they couldn't get him to take off his cap inside the hall. He also had the unfortunate impediment of singing a semitone higher than everyone else and, as he sang with great zeal, the rest of the congregation found his contribution to the service a little disconcerting. Barney hated those Sundays when his brother put on his uniform and would say, 'How much more Blood and Fire have I got to put up with.'

Because Freddie liked getting dressed up it wasn't long before someone thought that he would make an ideal Father Christmas. Unlike Barney, he loved children and could easily enter into their world of make-believe. Wasn't unreality often better than reality? When asked if he would like to be that year's Father Christmas at the

Christmas Bazaar he thought it was the greatest compliment the town could have paid him and couldn't wait to try on the long red cloak and beard.

He was told to collect his outfit from the Salvation Army Hall on the Wednesday morning before the Saturday, so that he could get used to it. The trouble was, he had not shared his honour, excitement, or secret with his brother because he knew very well that Barney would make fun of him in that, too.

Freddie put the large carrier-bag containing the cloak, wig and beard, down by the side of his armchair in the sitting-room, then went back to finishing his milk-round. He noticed his brother at the bottom of the yard brushing down an old wash-stand that someone wanted but decided that he would wait until he came back for his dinner before telling him about the Father Christmas job. Barney did whatever basic cooking was needed for their meals and Freddie did the shopping and washing-up. It was an arrangement that they had agreed upon after their parents died and would remain unchanged until only one of them was left to run the business.

For the rest of that morning Freddie was heard calling joyously 'It's a nice day, so far!' and 'Have you fed the baby, missis?' He became so involved in the part he was to play on Saturday that when he called 'Milko!' he added 'Father Christmas's here.'

When Barney went into the house to put the saucepan on the kitchen stove and to make up the sitting-room fire, he saw the brown carrier-bag by the side of his brother's chair. It was not unusual. Freddie occasionally brought back parcels of jumble from some of his customers who wanted to get rid of old clothes. Their rag-and-bone business didn't handle much of it because, as Barney always said, 'old coats only harbour new moths' but they sorted it out just in case something of value had been left in any of the pockets. The best was put to one side for another merchant who called about every two months, the rest was burnt.

Seeing the carrier-bag there reminded Barney that it was about time that Zacky Shufflebottom called on them. He cunningly managed a visit just before Christmas, if only to get a glass of free whisky which Barney kept in the sideboard for special occasions. They received little in return from Zacky, no more than a few shillings for a cartload of other people's cast-offs that had cost pounds.

Barney finished making up the fire and turned to go back into the kitchen. As he did so he stopped to pick up the carrier-bag and caught glimpses of what he thought was a red dress or overcoat. He threw the bag into a shed outside and returned to cooking the stew which they were going to have for dinner.

As Freddie made his way home he worried over how he was going to tell his brother about Saturday and being Father Christmas. He had to break the news somehow but could already hear Barney's derisive laughter.

He propped his trades-bike up against the shed door, went into the kitchen and washed his hands under the tap, then tiptoed into the sitting-room to make sure that the carrier-bag was still there.

Suddenly his simple joy turned to anger and when simple-minded men become angry their wrath can be frightening. He picked up a knife from the dining-table and went roaring into the kitchen.

'Where's my bag? Where's my Father Christmas outfit? Where…?'

Barney had just come in from the yard and said, 'What the hell's the matter with you?'

'Where is it? What've you done with my things?' yelled Freddie, slashing at the air with the knife which was pointing at his brother.

'What things? What's got into you?'

'You had no right to touch it. It was private.'

'Nothing's private in this house, you stupid bugger, so put that knife down.'

Freddie stepped nearer. 'Where is it? Where's my carrier-bag?'

Barney raised a clenched fist and shook it in Freddie's face.

'Put that knife down, I said. Then maybe I'll tell you where your carrier-bag is. It's in the shed with all the other junk you've brought home, waiting for Zacky to call.'

Freddie's anger was almost spent. He pushed past Barney and went to retrieve his borrowed property. There it was. The beard and wig had fallen out and now looked like the rest of the sad, discarded jumble. He picked them up, pulled the red cloak from its bag and examined them. They were all make-believe. Amongst all that rubbish the magic, the excitement and the beauty had gone out of them.

He could never tell his brother now. He put them all back into the carrier-bag and took them into the house.

'I promised to take these round to the Salvation Army Captain this afternoon,' he said. 'You just don't care, do you!'

Then he broke down and wept like a child.

14   A Ballad of the Bethlehem Donkey

One night I came to a stable
Half-hidden in the snow
And heard the roof-beams creaking
As the wild winds blew.

I walked towards the leaning door,
More scared than I can say,
When quietly from the shadows
A donkey spoke to me.

You've come, he said, *to see the Child,
The Holy Baby, the Christ?*
I trembled worse than if I'd heard
My own inquiring ghost.

How do you speak, at last I asked,
In words reserved for kings?
Tonight, he said, *for His dear sake
I have the gift of tongues.*

Where am I then and what strange thing
Is happening so late?
The inn was full, I only meant
To rest here till daylight.

*The inn was full for God's own Son
And so, among the straw,
His mother bore Him like a lamb
By the light of that star.*

Then angels gave me powers of speech
For this one blessed eve,
That I might tell to all wise men
Where truth is found, and love.

But why a donkey, why a crib,
And why this draughty stall?
Why not a bed with linen white
Or a well-lit hospital?

And tell me why you smile with joy
Yet weep salt tears as well,
Why shepherds kneel before the Child
And not some Cardinal?

I smile because I bear the crown
That kings will come to bless,
And weep because upon my back
I wear the shadow of a cross.

I know before that Babe grows old
He'll die for all of us.
So come with me, give praise to God,
Sing GLORIA IN EXCELSIS.

I entered in and saw the look
In those unearthly eyes,
They spoke of love and sorrow too,
Of all that was and ever is.

They spoke to me, they spoke my name.
I felt my blood run cold
To see within that winter barn
The Saviour of the world.

And there beside His makeshift cot
Among the meagre straw,
A woman sat wrapped in a rug
She'd borrowed from the poor.

She rocked her Son, she kissed His brow,
She knew one task was done,
Then felt upon His gentle flesh
The imprint of a thorn.

I never see a stable now
Without I see that face
And hear again the donkey sing
GLORIA IN EXCELSIS, FOR ALL OF US,
　　　　　　　　FOR ALL OF US.

15   As a Tale that is Told

I think I have to say, before I get too far into this story, that we had all once been supporters of Oliver Cromwell in those early days. He understood the fenmen and was behind us in our opposition to the land being drained. When he lived in Huntingdon – and later when he came to live in Ely – he always acted in our interests. He could see that in draining the Fens only the Gentlemen Adventurers (as they were called) and the King, would profit by it. You take water away from a fen man and he's lost. We could see our great meres disappearing and with them would go our fishing rights, our wild-fowling and our reed-growing. We were not, by nature, farmers. We tended to live by our wits. The waters helped to protect us, helped to preserve our independence – even Hereward knew that. There were times, of course, when the rivers burst their banks, when the floods washed us out of our homes, but we were still free men. We always were, from the very beginning, against interference from outside and had no great respect for whoever sat on the throne of England. Cromwell knew all that and spoke up for us. His enemies dubbed him 'Lord of the Fens', which was meant as an insult. Most people beyond our boundaries thought us a race of crude, uncouth law-breakers. But we trusted him, which is why so many fenmen volunteered to join his model army.

Promises! We should never trust a politician's promises whichever side he's on. It seems to me that they're all out to feather their own nests and Cromwell was no exception.

Power! The temptations are so great. Ambitions, once

they are in full flood, cannot be quelled any more than we could stop our swollen rivers from bursting.

Cromwell soon forgot his promises and, in the end, we learnt to our sorrow that he had betrayed us. But, I have to say, we also betrayed ourselves. We were forced to then, if we wanted to survive. After all, when I was a young man I was opposed to draining the Fens like everyone else. Yet I ended up working as a dyker, a navvy working under the Dutchman, Vermuyden. He was a hard man – at least, the men under him were, the gangers and landowners who wanted their pound of flesh. They thrashed us as readily as they thrashed their horses – worse sometimes.

It was hard work digging those long drains. Miles and miles of mud, sludge, clay and gravel which had to be dug out by hand, often in the foulest weather. Most of us were used to working in water, used to the cold winds that blew across that flat, bleak land. But we did it in our own time. Digging the dykes nearly broke our backs and I've seen some poor devils just fall face down in the mud and not bother to get up again. We may have volunteered to fight in Cromwell's army but few of us went willingly to dig for the drainers. Most of us were sent, often as a punishment for some petty criminal offence, like poaching. I suppose it was better than being sent to jail, or whipped round the town and laughed at by the gentry.

I was arrested for taking part in a political demonstration. The magistrates said I was disturbing the peace, which came close to treason. All we thought we were doing was protesting in the market-place against the rising price of flour and the cost of bread.

It had been a terrible winter. There was no work, no trade for any fish or fowl we caught. And there was illness in the Fens, too. Children were dying for want of food. We had to do something.

But the troops were called out from Cambridge and more than eighty of us were arrested. The ringleaders were jailed for twenty years. The rest of us were ordered to work for the drainers, for one shilling a week for five years.

It was during my last year that I decided to get married.

It had to be more or less in secret and on one of the few days I had off – Christmas Day. Our village parson was a kind man, fond of brandy and a fat goose or young swan. Quite a lot of fine brandy found its way into the Fens and there was never any problem in snaring a goose or poaching a good hive of eels.

It was after supplying our parson with some of these delicacies that I asked if he would marry us. He knew my sweetheart from his frequent visits to Sir Wilburton Coles's house where she worked as a laundry maid. He thought I had made a good match but said, 'Is there already a loaf in the basket, Jackson?' meaning, was she pregnant? and I said no, certainly not.

We were married at half-past eight in the morning with just two witnesses and nobody else there. The church was bitterly cold but we had the full service, then went into the vestry to make our marks in the register. After that the parson gave us each a glass of brandy. Although I was pretty certain it wasn't his first of the day, it was mine and I can remember how it burned in my stomach like liquid fire. What with being cold and hungry I felt as if I'd swallowed hot coals. I was more accustomed to home-made beers than spirits but I soon got used to it and drank the whole glass. My wife could manage no more than a few sips so the parson finished hers. Then we walked home to begin our married life together in a small wooden, single-storeyed house half-way between the village and the river-bank where I was working.

As soon as my wife's mistress – Lady Millicent – found out she dismissed her on the spot and we had to make do as best as we could.

It was while I was walking home one day from my work that I met an old man on the road. I could see immediately that he was not one of your typical beggers, of which there were many on the roads then. He was fairly well clothed and had a good pair of boots. He wore a brown cloak and carried a staff cut from an ash tree. He would have been about fifty, though, with his white hair and limp, he looked older. He told me he was a travelling preacher, trying to bring the true teachings of Christ to ordinary people who saw the established Church as a symbol of wealth, greed, intolerance and injustice. Those were the views shared by most fen men, I told him, and they had landed most of us in trouble.

'So I have heard,' he said. 'But do they know what it should really be like? You cannot blame Christ if his church is now corrupt. Do you not think he would over-turn the tables of the money-lenders today if he were to return to our midst?'

We walked on and I asked him if he was staying in the village, and where. He had no plans. 'I shall find a room somewhere,' he said. 'If not, I shall not be the first.' And his grey face suddenly broke into a smile. 'I assume there is an inn in the village?'

I told him there was but that it was a rough place frequented by navvies from the drainage works who did their best to get drunk and then fought each other before falling into the arms of some waiting harlot.

'What is a navvy?' he asked.

'It's the nickname given to the men who are navigating the new drains across the fens. Some of us are called dykers. We're a mixed crew. Scottish, Dutch, as well as local men. The Scots were originally brought down as prisoners-of-war, so were the Dutch. Quite a lot of them stayed. It was work. They like to think they can drink the English into oblivion but fail to realize that you certainly can't do that to a fen man, or 'fen-tykers' as the Dutch call us – which is why some people now call us 'fen-tigers'. It's a miserable existence, I can tell you. There are times when I wonder what life is for.'

He slowly shook his head. 'Man that is born of woman hath but a short time to live and is full of misery! saith the scriptures. You are familiar with those words I am sure.' He went on to quote more: 'As for man, his days are as grass; as a flower of the field so he flourisheth. For the wind passeth over it and it is gone; and the place thereof shall know it no more.'

We reached our house and I suggested he could spend the night with us if he didn't mind sleeping on the floor in front of the kitchen fire. He hesitated for a moment, smiled graciously, and accepted.

My wife, who was then pregnant, had been baking. The house smelt warm and spicy from the newly made cakes. She was a good cook, a wonderful homemaker, and I was proud of her. Although nervous on our arrival she accepted our guest with a friendly welcome. From her years in service with Lady Millicent Coles, she knew what to do and the preacher was treated as an old friend who had been expected for days.

After our meal he sat and talked to us in a quiet, lilting voice. He called himself a preacher but, to me, he was more like a prophet. He said:

Things will change. Whether all those changes will be for the better is doubtful. There will be some good, some bad. We spend our years as a tale that is told, as the psalmist says. Our lives are so brief we never see the whole plan. You will know sorrow and joy, hardship and comfort. Thrones will fall and new kingdoms be established. Your children and their children will inherit a different world, where men are more equal, where their faith will be free to declare itself, where food is more plentiful and where men will be allowed to rest from their labours for more than one day a year. But there will also be wars and pestilences, hatred and starvation for no matter how long man lives he will never learn that love and generosity of spirit are worth more than all the world's riches. Greed will always be our downfall for the love of possessions leads us to other vices. I preach goodness but I am also aware that evil is just as powerful. It is like the water in your rivers, or this fire in your hearth. Both can comfort and provide. Both, if unguarded, can break out and destroy.

He could see that we were very tired and in need of sleep. He thanked us for our hospitality, gave us a blessing, then, as we went off to our room he settled himself down on the kitchen floor.

When we woke up in the morning the fire was remade

and blazing brightly but the stranger had gone. The small loaf of bread that my wife had put ready for breakfast had been broken into portions and a small wooden cross was left on the pewter plate he had used.

I went out into the road to see if he was within eyes' reach but there was no sign of him. For a few moments I felt insulted, thinking that he had crept off like that without saying thank you. But then I assumed he had his own reasons for this quiet departure and would not have wanted my wife to pack him a meal for the road. He had expressed his gratitude for shelter in a more practical way. When I stepped back into the house it was as if he was still there.

Although my wife and I often spoke of this incident within our own walls, we did not mention it to anyone else. The months passed by and on 6 December our first child was born – a son of robust health and robust lungs. Eighteen months later, on 13 July, we had a daughter and a year after that another son.

Having more than served my sentence as a dyker I found work on the land that had been reclaimed from the water and became a farm-hand. The land now belonged to the Earl of Bedford, who had cottages built for his workers, and so we moved house. The years of joy that the preacher had promised were upon us. Seven years in all. Life was better than we'd expected.

But then another stranger arrived in the village, this time a merchant from the city, selling wool. It was good Flemish wool and the women were eager to buy. It was not all that he brought. News had already reached us of the plague in London and other large cities but we never thought it would ever find its way into the Fens. It was terrible to see people stricken down with it so quickly. Hardly a house was untouched. A field at the back of the church was turned into a graveyard specially for those who died of it, for there were those who would not have the bodies buried within the churchyard itself. The funeral bell seldom stopped tolling. I followed my own two sons to that field and have grieved for them ever since. My cup of sorrow had, I thought, been more than filled.

My wife and daughter were spared, thank God, until last year when my wife died. And that was one of the cruellest ironies that fate could have devised for she was buried on Christmas Day, just as we had been married on Christmas Day thirty years earlier. My world had changed all right. So had everyone else's I suppose. As the preacher had said, our 'days are as grass'.

Fortunately my daughter Sophie lives only a few miles away in the village of Geesely. She has three children now and has asked me to go and spend Christmas with them. I said I wouldn't, at first, but she kept insisting. 'You need cheering up,' she said. 'If you're so fond of quoting the bible for goodness sake try to find something that's not so depressing.'

I said the scriptures were written to make us think, not to make us laugh.

'Then why does the good book tell us to go our ways, to eat our bread with joy, and to drink our wine with a merry heart?'

I couldn't answer that and smiled at Sophie taking me on at my own game.

When I walked into her kitchen on Christmas morning there was a lovely smell of newly baked bread, spiced cakes, and a fine capon turning on the spit.

16   *The Watcher at the Gate*

Harry Preston had been head verger at Anglebury Cathedral for seventeen years and this was to be his last Christmas before retirement.

His house in the close was next to the Norman Gateway and faced the tall, impressive west front of a building that had been his daily place of work as well as worship.

It would not be easy to give up a view like that to go and live in a modern bungalow on a small estate, away from the slow pace and sense of history he had known for so long.

He had chosen a bungalow because his wife, Agnes, was now much crippled with arthritis and would soon need a wheel-chair. The artificial hip replacement she'd had last year had only partially helped and she now found it difficult to get up and down the stairs of their present house. But, as she frequently said to her friends, it was worth the effort just to have such a wonderful view from their bedroom window, especially on a morning like this when the close had received its first fall of snow and the cathedral rose even more majestically from its surroundings.

'Doesn't it look beautiful, Harry?' she said, when she struggled over to draw back the curtains. 'Pure and unspoilt. There are no tyre marks on the road yet, only one set of footprints going across the green – Horace Sawtry's no doubt, he seems to be showing a little more enthusiasm these days.'

Horace Sawtry was the present second verger, hoping to gain promotion when Harry retired in March. He lived

on the north-east side of the close and his wife, Mildred, was equally keen to move into the house near the gateway because 'it had more status'.

Agnes turned back towards her bed. 'This weather's come just right for the Dean's Christmas party tonight,' she said. 'You will go, won't you Harry, for my sake!'

'I've told you, love, I just don't like the thought of going without you. I'd much rather stay at home. I'll not be missed.'

'But you will. Besides you can't miss this year. It may well be your last chance. You mustn't stay away on my account. In any case, I shall want to hear all the gossip when you get back.'

He knew he had no other choice but did not like the thought of leaving Agnes on her own. Normally he was able to get someone to sit with her but this year, for the first time, nearly everybody had been invited to the party.

Harry had known many changes during his seventeen years as verger. He had watched people come and go, he had been part of many historic moments in the cathedral, had witnessed the enthronements of three bishops and had attended to royalty, but there had never been so many immediate changes as those introduced by the new dean during his first twelve months in office.

The close was changing too. Once most of the houses had been for the clergy and lay clerks. Now the residents represented a much wider section of society because the houses had been converted into flats which were rented by single teachers, solicitors' clerks, accountants, nurses and retired spinsters. Admittedly some tenants, such as Miss Maggie Whitbread and Miss Edith Waterman, had lived in the close for many years but others, like Penny Crampton and Rodney Street had been there no longer than a year or two.

There were also people like Mrs Cynthia Rippingill – a wealthy widow who had come to live in the close and was now exercising considerable influence on those around her, and little Rosie Campkin who had been housekeeper to the late Archdeacon Wallace and was allowed one of the smaller flats at a very small rent. To show her gratitude she attended Evensong every day without fail.

It was customary during the last two weeks that led up to Christmas for most of the tenants to receive invitations to one or other of the annual 'at home' parties that were part of the close's social pattern. One's position in the community would determine which of these parties one would be invited to attend. They were always organized in the same order, starting with Canon and Mrs Vincent-Smith, then Canon Laurence Jessup and his wife Penelope, continuing with Dr Malcolm Skipton, Master of Music, then Mrs Rippingill, culminating in the one given by the dean.

In previous years, by the time the parties had reached that stage, invitations had become very selective and guests felt privileged to be among the favoured few. Even so, these occasions were still highly competitive and comparisons made as to where they served the best mulled wine, made the tastiest mince-pies, and had the most pretentious display of Christmas cards – which was simply another way of disguising one's jealousy.

Since her husband's death five years ago Mrs Rippingill had firmly established herself as the first lady of the close. Her father had been a well-known farmer in an area of the Fens particularly well-known for its wealthy farmers, and her husband had been a popular accountant specializing in matters concerning the Inland Revenue Office on behalf of the wealthy farmers, all of whom, she frequently declared, had 'known hard times'.

In addition to her Christmas parties Mrs Rippingill organized several sherry mornings each year. An invitation to one of these almost demanded that one had an OBE, or had won the Nobel Prize for physics or literature – it didn't matter which as long as one was another name to drop somewhere else.

Harry Preston, for instance, had never been invited to one of Mrs Rippingill's 'at home' parties even though each week he escorted her to her pew in the choir-stalls. He was an employee and too lowly.

The precentor, the Reverend Dawson Pyke, had only just reached that social peak and he had been at Anglebury Cathedral now for four years. His disadvantage – or disqualification – was that he rode a motor-bike, which Mrs Rippingill considered much too common and undignified for a clergyman in his position. 'I can remember,' she would say in tones of regret and scorn, 'when all the Chapter had their own carriages and grooms.'

Those days belonged to the era of Dean Leefold Robinson, who wore gaiters and gave orders in a voice as near to divine authority as one could possibly get on earth.

His successor – Dean Richard Pointer – came from a very different cut of the cloth. He had spent several years as a parish priest in the north of England and had no time for snobbery. He did not enjoy living in the flat landscape of the Fens, nor did he approve of the stuffy attitudes surrounding his new job. He wanted to break down the class barriers and dispense with some of the old traditions so that his cathedral could be seen as one of the most up-to-date in the country.

Everyone was intrigued about the deanery party that year as all and sundry would be there – from the mighty to the lowly, from the believers to the unbelievers. As well as the bishop, the dean had also invited the gardeners, the chapter clerk, the vergers and their wives, plus Maggie Whitbread, Penny Crampton and Rodney Street who was putting up as a Labour candidate in the next local elections.

As well as the traditional mulled wine, there was draught beer, soft drinks and cocktails. Instead of the customary canapés served on silver trays by uniformed servants, the dean's two teenage daughters went round with plates of sandwiches, slices of pork-pie, jacket potatoes and home-made pickles.

Sybil Pointer, the dean's wife, was an equally happy-go-lucky person who liked to be where the fun was. 'Don't stand on ceremony,' she announced loudly. 'You'll find plenty of butter on the sideboard and if you want a fork you'll probably find one in the kitchen.'

Cynthia Rippingill and Penelope Jessup sipped their white wine and looked on in amazement. 'Christmas used to be so different in dear Dean Robinson's day, didn't it!' said Mrs Rippingill. 'In those days we believed in gracious living and certain standards. But now, well, just look how some people dress. You would think their wardrobes came from a jumble sale, not that I know what a jumble sale really is. Why is it, Penelope, that people no longer have any taste or breeding?'

Before Penelope could reply Mrs Rippingill had taken another breath and continued with her assessment of the human race. 'It seems to be quite ridiculous for these people to blame the government or to talk about recession and hardship. They know nothing about it. Now, in the

Thirties it was different. There we were, growing thousands of tons of potatoes and no one would buy them. We just had to plough them in. My poor father didn't know where to put himself. He almost went bankrupt, you know. Would have done if it had not been for the war.'

Mrs Jessup was grateful to see that her husband had just joined the small circle captively listening to Cynthia's tirade. But even his arrival did not stop the flow of pompous comments and complaints about the rest of the world, including the Church.

'Ah, Laurence, I am pleased you are here because I want to know why all these new-fangled services are still being foisted on us when we don't like them! I am utterly confused with all your Rite A's, Rite B's and C's, or whatever you call them. Isn't the *Book of Common Prayer* good enough any more, or can't your new young ordinands understand it?'

Canon Jessup, like his wife, attempted to intervene but to no avail. He only managed to say, 'But Cynthia, the Synod authorized the A.S.B. ...' and she was off again. 'Oh how I loathe this modern use of initials for everything these days. *A.S.B.* It could mean anything – The Amalgamated Society of Brewers, or Boiler-makers ...'

'Or Bookies?' said Laurence Jessup, as he finally laughed Mrs Rippingill into submission, if not silence.

To the relief of everyone the dean called for order by loudly ringing a handbell and announcing that it was time for some carols.

In Dean Robinson's day it had always been the custom to end the party with a group of choristers standing on the stairs, singing carols by candlelight while the guests listened. For Mrs Rippingill it had always been the highlight of the evening.

This year was to be different. The dean invited everyone to gather round the piano for a community-style sing-song. Already in his shirt sleeves and wearing a paper-hat, he sat at the keyboard and thumped out an introduction to *The First Nowell* that suggested he might have learnt his technique as a taproom pianist in The Pig and Whistle. The response, to begin with, was a little restrained and he demanded much more gusto for *God Rest Ye, Merry, Gentlemen*.

Harry Preston, who had spent the evening moving about from group to group without attaching himself to anyone in particular, looked on with amazement and disbelief. He, too, had known the more elegant days of Dean Leefold Robinson and was not at all sure what to make of the new regime and its idea of 'a classless society'. He would certainly have plenty to tell Agnes when he returned home, if she was still awake. He looked at his watch. It was already eleven-thirty.

The community singing continued for another three carols and then the dean asked everyone to be quiet for a moment as he had a special treat for them. All the lights were switched off so that only the candles on the window-sills and Christmas tree glowed in the room. In view of the dean's unorthodox approach to most things the guests wondered what was going to happen next.

At that moment the great oak door that led into the hall and stair-well opened and there, on the stairs, stood twenty choristers, robed in red, some holding lanterns, all looking as angelic as Mrs Rippingill could have wished.

At a signal from their master of music, Doctor Skipton, they began to sing *In the Bleak Midwinter*. The purity of sound after the noisy sing-song round the piano, was ethereal. The setting could not have been more theatrical or timely. It was as if one of the Christmas cards had come to life. Harry felt a lump rise in his throat and he wished that Agnes could have been there for that moment if nothing else.

The boys then sang *Ding Dong Merrily on High, Past Three o'Clock, Away in a Manger* and *We Wish You a Merry Christmas*. When the lights were switched on again it was as if everyone had been transported to a time and a place where there was no poverty or pretence, no starvation or wealth, no snobbery or doubt. Even Mrs Rippingill was subdued and, when she left, thanked the dean profusely for a wonderful party that had kept alive 'those time-honoured customs we all love here at Anglebury'.

Harry walked home alone through the close to his house, towards the small lighted window near the gateway where he knew that Agnes would still be waiting to hear a description of all that had happened. The snow had hardened under the night's frost. Behind him the great west front of the cathedral stood floodlit and aloof from all the trivial affairs that were so important in the lives of a community that still remained isolated from the busy life of the city outside its walls.

As he reached his front gate he turned and looked back at a thousand years of history in stone. And, he thought, but for a humble birth two thousand years ago, it would not even be there. It was all still a mystery, requiring a lot of faith.

It was just as hard to believe that this was going to be his last Christmas there as a cathedral verger. Although it was always his busiest time of the year, with all the extra services and concerts, he still loved it and couldn't help wondering how he would feel in a year's time when he was no longer part of it.

Standing there for those few moments, as he did so often at the end of the day, he knew that the deanery party was already fading into insignificance, as a cloud slipping towards the horizon. The stillness was disturbed only briefly by a few distant voices as some of the other guests made their way home. Then all was silent again.

He wanted to move but could not. It was as if he had been frozen in time, as if all the clocks had stopped and the earth itself had ceased breathing. Why, he wondered, do some moments appear to last a lifetime, whilst seventeen years shrink into an hour?

Like someone waking from sleep he felt for the key in his pocket. If he didn't go in now and tell Agnes all about the party before she went to sleep he knew he would have forgotten most of it by the morning.

The cathedral clock began to chime midnight. He waited until the last stroke died away, then went indoors.

17   *The Song of Mary*

There was always the waiting.
After the message from Gabriel
How could I share my knowledge
With anyone I knew? I was not able
To explain the mystery in my womb
Or let my neighbours see too soon
What they could never understand.
Some people always think the worst
Even of those they know. How could I boast
That I was mothering God's son?
His child was not the only thing I nursed.

And then there was the waiting
From Nazareth to Bethlehem –
Not the best time for a woman
To be travelling. With every breath
There came another loneliness, for birth,
I found, is very like a death.
We arrived too late that afternoon
To find a room and had to sleep
On straw provided by the keeper of an inn,
Our only light a lantern's flame
Glowing beside the manger, like a sun.

There was another waiting then
Until my child was born and men
From off the hills came down to see
If what the angels said was true.
And there he lay, smiling as if he knew
Why they had left their sheep to kneel

Before him round a cattle stall.
But I felt nervous should the news
Bring visitors less welcome.
Not everyone looked kindly on the Jews
And we were strangers far from home.

Yet, there were other waitings
Which I did not mind. Three wise men
Bearing gifts came from the east
And stood in wonder at what they found,
Thinking the child would be an earthly king
In some grand room above the ground.
My aching then was deeper wrung
With pride, when what I should have known
Was calm humility. He was my son
And not my son. What mother cannot bring
Herself to ponder on what birth has done?

Some waitings are unbearable
As waiting must have been for Simeon.
But mine was worse because I knew
My child had left me when his eyes
Looked heavenward. The more he grew
The less I saw him as my own.
I felt the pain stab in my heart.
The blood I'd shed for him would soon
Be shed for others. I thought my part
In the story almost done. I gave him life
But did not know such joy could turn to grief.

Then longer waitings told me otherwise.
There was a Calvary, and there were tears.
But if I could begin his birth again
I would, for over all the years
His love has reached beyond the cross
To bless all those who, following a star,
Have stood before that stable door.
I've watched their eyes fill with his light
And shared the peace within each heart.
For I, who gave that child his breath,
Know how the world was changed that night.

18   An Uninvited Guest

The 400-year-old house stood in the middle of the Fens, in what is still known as The Bedford Level, named after the Earls of Bedford who, in the seventeenth century, were largely responsible for raising the capital needed by Sir Cornelius Vermuyden for his ambitious drainage project. The house had once belonged to one of his overseers and was eventually named after the Dutchman who frequently stayed there.

Vermuyden House was a large, stone building that could have been mistaken for a small Elizabethan manor. It had an impressive flight of stone steps leading up to the front porch and its great roof was crowned with twelve ornate chimneys.

I came to know the house well because for several years I and a group of musical friends were invited by the Love family to present an evening of Christmas entertainment there, to which they invited their friends and people from neighbouring villages. There was always a gathering of about forty guests and the evenings were the kind of delightful occasion at which Charles Dickens or Jane Austen would not have been out of place. We never had such distinguished personages there, of course, but we liked to feel that we had put the clocks back far enough to enjoy an event that would have been familiar to them.

Our concerts always took place in a large drawing-room with a magnificent fireplace at each end. There were chandeliers, gilt-framed mirrors, life-size portraits, a grand piano and, for this Christmas programme, as many armchairs and sofas as the room could accommodate.

There was also a large, real Christmas tree, a plentiful supply of logs on each hearth and, from the kitchen, the mouthwatering smell of hot mince-pies and the vapours of mulled wine.

But, before these could be served, there was the customary entertainment – a Yuletide soirée, from the musicians and readers, followed by some carol singing with the guests. We tried to do something different each year and, because we knew that this year there would be one or two visitors from overseas, we chose to present *A Christmas Journey Round the World*. We had collected some interesting accounts of what Christmas was like in Sweden, France, Poland, Italy and Russia. We had chosen carols from Czechoslovakia, Spain and Mexico, as well as the traditional English ones. Whatever a country's history or political regime might be, we soon discovered that nearly every nation in the world celebrated some form of Christmas, from South America to Finland, from Alaska to Australia – a hundred different cultures colouring a simple story in their own way. Not that it's all that simple when you stop to think about it. Nothing ever is.

About a quarter of a mile from Vermuyden House was one of the main drains that his dykers had cut in the seventeenth century. That, too, had its history. When it was decided by the Crown and the Gentlemen Adventurers to drain the Fens, the local people (not surprisingly) resented the idea. It threatened their very existence. They had felt that they were safely out of harm's way, surviving quite well with their wild-fowling, fishing and reed-beds, and saw no reason at all why their livelihood should be destroyed to provide a few wealthy aristocrats with more land. They not only refused to work for Vermuyden, they sabotaged much of his work as soon as it was finished.

As the Dutchman could not raise a sufficient labour force from the local people, he had to import enforced labour, such as the Scottish prisoners-of-war who were brought down to the Fens to dig his dykes through this strange flat land. Some of these dykes were more than twenty miles long and had to be dug out manually, mile after mile, often in terrible weather and always under the eyes of ruthless masters. The foremen, or 'gangers' as they were called, ruled by the authority of the whip. If any of the men failed to respond to that correction they were then punished in the stocks and deprived of their food. Those who failed to submit to those disciplines were transported or sentenced to death.

As the local people were so opposed to the drainage and so determined to destroy the work done by the drainers, the gangers decided to employ some of their ex-soldiers to guard each day's achievements. It is part of fenland folklore now that one night the men from a nearby village, armed with clubs, cleavers and eel-glaives, crept up to where the prisoners were on duty and savagely murdered them. When their comrades found their bodies in the morning they put a curse on that particular fen and vowed revenge. As far as we know nothing ever came of their threat and the fen has flourished. But, there was an old woman, many years ago, who claimed that she had seen the ghosts of those two soldiers walking the fields. Naturally, it wasn't long before her story became a legend that was told in the neighbouring pubs on winter evenings by men who had the fen men's art of making a drama out of an anecdote.

However, I must not digress. All this is incidental to the account I am supposed to be giving of our Christmas concert at Vermuyden House – though, when I look back now I can't help feeling that we were destined to be part of what happened. It was as if everything about that night was touched by forces beyond our control.

It had started to snow at four o'clock and I was wondering whether this was going to threaten our twelve-mile journey into the Fens in some three hours time. Usually I am pleased to see snow. As well as the purity of whiteness that it brings I like also the stillness. It gives the impression that everything it touches has been told to stop breathing, as if the earth has been put into a kind of trance. But on this occasion I had mixed feelings about it. If we had no more than an inch or two then it would simply give us the perfect setting for our evening, creating an atmosphere that words could not equal. If we had several inches, then our journey on narrow, unlit roads could become a nightmare. There is little margin for error between fen roads and their dykes in ideal conditions but when the grass verge is hidden by snow each road becomes doubly treacherous. Fortunately we were in luck and by five o'clock the snow had stopped. The low, grey clouds had moved on, leaving us with a spacious, starlit sky that later allowed a frost to gild the whiteness of the earth.

When we arrived at the house most of the guests were already there, enjoying a glass of punch. We each accepted a glass to wish everyone the compliments of the season, then went off to a smaller room to change into our evening wear. By eight o'clock our hosts and the audience were ready for the concert to begin. The main lights were switched off, leaving only candles burning round the room and on the tree.

We started with a French carol, then flitted from country to country, with stories about St Lucia in Sweden, St Nicholas in Poland, or the native Indians on the shores of Quebec in 1620 singing their carol *Jesus, Ahatonhia!* Our readings were interspersed with solos and musical items – piano, guitar and recorder.

It was all going very well until we heard a scream from upstairs and one of Mr and Mrs Love's children came rushing down to say that she had seen a strange man on the landing. The response from the guests was mixed. Some laughed and thought it a joke; others said she must have been dreaming, whilst others – especially her parents – believed the child to be truly frightened.

When asked what the man looked like she said that he was not very tall and was wearing unusual clothes. She thought he also had reddish hair.

Her father went upstairs and searched every room but could find no trace of any intruder. All the windows and doors were still fastened and it would have been impossible for anyone to have gone up the stairs without passing through the drawing-room or kitchen.

'But I definitely saw him,' she sobbed, imploring us to

believe her. 'He looked at me. He had very sad eyes. It was as if he was staring right through me. I know he was there.'

Her father returned and shrugged his shoulders. 'Well, Susie, I know you've got a good imagination but I can assure you there's no one there. You probably saw a shadow, or dreamt you saw something.'

'I didn't,' she said quietly. 'Anyway, I'm not going back to my room until you come to bed.'

She went to sit on the arm of the chair next to her mother and we were asked to continue with the rest of the programme. Our journey round the world was bringing us closer to home with some English carols and a reading from Thomas Hardy's *Under the Greenwood Tree*. I was just about to follow this with his poem *The Oxen* when we all heard a very unusual sound – the sound of bagpipes.

Everyone became tense and listened. The music was coming from one of the upstairs rooms. It grew louder, then faded, before becoming louder again, as if the player was slowly walking backwards and forwards on the landing before disappearing once more into a room.

I recognized the tune as an old Scottish folk-song and began to sing the words to the pipes' accompaniment. I motioned to the guests to remain still and made my way slowly to the stairs. Then I saw what Susie had seen. The figure of a man in a kilt, moving towards me on the landing, a man with reddish hair. He knew that I had seen him and, in that instance, vanished.

I didn't know how I was going to convince Mr and Mrs Love that their house was haunted but it surely was. Nor did I want to frighten the guests any more than they already were. They had all heard the sounds. Several asked me if I had seen anything. One or two suggested that we should ring the police.

There was no point in trying to continue with the concert and so I proposed that we should all relax, if only to do justice to the wonderful Yuletide refreshments that were ready to be served. Then, if anyone still wanted to sing a few carols before going home, we would be happy to oblige.

I took Mr Love to one side and told him what I had seen. 'You don't have to explain,' he said calmly, 'I do know it's there. I've kept it to myself for a long time and thought perhaps that last year we had seen the last of him.'

'Him? Who do you think he is, then?'

'I am convinced that it's one of the Scottish prisoners-of-war who was murdered in the seventeenth century whilst working for Cornelius Vermuyden. *Vermuyden House!* Where else would he want to haunt? That's one of the reasons why I'm thinking of moving.' He told me that his wife, Sarah, also knew of the ghost's existence and that they had always tried to protect their children from the truth. 'But you can see now, it's impossible. Not that the poor chap means us any harm. I'm sure he doesn't.'

I took a long sip of my mulled wine. 'It seems a pity to let him drive you out of your home. How many visitations do you get?'

'We can't be sure. Certainly no more than twice a year. For a couple of years we saw nothing at all.'

'You must have been hoping that he had gone back to Scotland.'

'No such luck.'

'But if he's harmless and his visits are so infrequent why are you thinking of giving up this lovely house?'

'You try living with a ghost – and two daughters. If they really *knew* he existed they'd leave home anyway.'

The phone in the hall started to ring and I turned to speak to some of the other guests. As I did so, the distant sound of lamenting pipes faded through the house and we all froze into silence. When the sound died away there was a sudden calm in the room and, as if with relief, we all simultaneously lifted our glasses to our lips and drank deeply.

Perhaps, at last, the Scottish soldier had decided to go home if not for Christmas then maybe for Hogmanay.

We drove home across the Fens, hardly able to believe that we had been present at an actual haunting. We had set out to create a world of make-believe, an imaginary journey through the legends of other countries, and we had been part of one ourselves. For the next few miles we were tempted to believe that every shadow we saw, every glimmer of light or unusual sound, was another voice from a troubled past.

The Love family did leave Vermuyden House, not because of its kilted spectre but because Roger Love had been offered an important job in America which he could not afford to turn down. The house remained empty for two or three years. Either no one could meet the asking price or its reputation was now too well known. Since then it has been turned into 'executive flats' and the sound of the pipes will never be heard there again.

I am not normally a superstitious person, but I have to admit that although we have given several Christmas concerts since that night, we have never given the same programme. I don't think we could without half expecting to hear again the wailing sound of the sad, wandering, homesick tune.

Sometimes I can't help thinking that there must be more than just two ghosts somewhere out there where our strange history has been made. On cold, bleak winter days, when I hear the wind scraping its throat on the sharp thorns of a hedge, or moaning in the telegraph wires that still stretch across the Fens, I believe it is trying to tell me something. Is it, perhaps, because I probably have Scottish blood in me, from an ancester who was brought down to dig those first dykes and never went back home?

Eventually I was prepared to put this experience as much out of my mind as possible but, the following winter I received a letter from a lady in Aberdeen who called herself 'an elderly student of genealogy' which proved to me that the matter was not yet over. After the customary introduction and explanation she went on to say:

For the past six years I have been trying to compile my family tree and have already established our lineage for several generations. For some branches of the family I have been able to trace our origins to the early sixteenth century, establishing not only dates of births, deaths and marriages, but also discovering that most of the adult males of our family had served in one or other of the Scottish regiments. Furthermore, most of them had been Pipe-majors. But, as usual, vital links are missing, such as relatives who were known to have existed and to have joined the army but for whom, as yet, I can find no other record. Quite recently I learned from one of your books of the Scottish soldiers who, as prisoners-of-war, were sent down to the Fens in the seventeenth century to provide a labour force for Cornelius Vermuyden. Is it possible that some of those early Drainage Board registers are kept in the county archives? If so I would be most grateful if you could make some enquiries for me, especially to see if there is by any chance a reference to a Sergeant-Major Sandy McIntyre, a piper captured at Dunbar. I am almost certain he did not return home, nor did he marry a local girl and settle in the Fens as some of his regiment did. Nor has his name appeared on any of the pension or discharge lists that I have examined. So you can see he is something of a mystery. Any help or information you can send me will be greatly appreciated and I enclose a stamped addressed envelope for your reply. With thanks.

Your sincerely,

(Mrs) Morag McInloch.

Was this all too much of a coincidence, or was I still destined to pursue the troubled ghost of Vermuyden House? My usual feelings are to let the dead rest in peace – if ever they do.

19   Touching the Stars

I could not believe he was blind until I moved slightly to one side to put my empty plate on a nearby table. In that moment I noticed that he went on talking as if I was still there in front of him. It disturbed me to see him addressing his remarks to a blank wall. What deceived me even more was that, although without sight, he wore glasses and his eyes appeared to be as lively as anyone's when enjoying an interesting conversation.

Within seconds, of course, I was back in front of him, continuing as if nothing had happened. But I could not forget his disadvantage and found myself choosing my words with more care. How easy it is to say, 'Did you by any chance see on television last night…?' or 'Hasn't that girl over there got lovely hair!'

We had met at a Christmas drinks party – one of those occasions where you stand around with a glass of wine in one hand, a plate of vol-au-vents in the other, and are then expected to shake hands with all the other guests and talk at the same time. As the evening progresses the noise level rises. Loud voices compete with shrill voices as all become aware that they are being drowned out by the background music which has become foreground within half an hour of one's arrival.

Our hosts were Keith and Liz Kilby – acquaintances rather than close friends, a lively couple who loved entertaining in their spacious house which had once been a rectory.

Keith introduced me to Philip Ball because he thought we probably shared an interest in Egyptology and astronomy. I was no expert but had been fascinated by both subjects since my late teens, some thirty-five years ago. Philip, too, was in his middle fifties I thought; a smart, dark-haired and handsome man – though I have long since learnt that men's ideas of handsomeness differ from those of the opposite sex. Philip lacked ruggedness and flair, presenting, to begin with, a sombre image. But I soon found him to be a witty man with a subtle sense of humour and quick to make a pun. He was married and several times during our conversation I saw his wife Laura glancing over towards us, just to make sure he was not in need of other company. They had been married for more than twenty years but had no family. I was still single.

Laura was a striking woman with good dress sense and a lively face. Even at a distance I could see that her eyes flashed with a curiosity that recorded more in five seconds than most people's would in five minutes. She appeared to notice everything and I couldn't help wondering if she had unconsciously developed the habit of trying to be two pairs of eyes, looking at things not only for herself but also for her husband. She was, I discovered later that evening, an accountant in the town and also honorary secretary to the local Talking Newspaper Association.

Before losing his eyesight in a motor-cycle accident twelve years previously, Philip had taught physics at a nearby Boys Grammar School, where he was also hoping to become the deputy head. The accident meant he had to make several adjustments to those ambitions and he now worked in the modern languages department, using his natural skills as a linguist to great effect. He was a popular teacher with the boys and became a regular supporter at their rugger matches.

I complimented him on being so accomplished in both the sciences and the arts, as well as liking sport.

'One was necessity, the other love,' he said. 'My father had always wanted to be a doctor but instead he became the manager of an insurance company. He insisted that I went in for sciences at school but my heart was never in them. I always wanted to travel and preferred to concentrate on languages. If I went to France I knew I'd want to speak French; if I went to Italy I would want to speak Italian, and so on. Then there was the literature. As a writer you must know what risks there are in translation. Flaubert or Maupassant in anything but French is like trying to smell a rose through a blanket.'

'So you teach French? Anything else?'

'A little German or Spanish, depending on what's needed. I would have liked to have learnt Russian but I think it's too late now. Tolstoy and Dostoyevsky in braille would be daunting enough.'

'With all these achievements how on earth did you find time for Egyptology and astronomy?'

'I thought that you would eventually get round to mentioning these. Keith told me that you were passionate about them.'

'That's a bit of an overstatement. Keen, maybe, but I am no expert.'

'Nor am I. For me they are simply interests left over from school. We were lucky enough to have a lovely, eccentric classics master who made me excited about the Ancient Egyptians and, through them, I developed an interest in the stars.'

'Were you drawn to any particular reign of the pharaohs?'

'I always felt some kind of affinity with Akhenaton, I suppose. And most men have drooled over Queen Nefertiti at some time in their lives. Haven't you? Remote and aloof though she always seemed. Even Hitler had a crush on her, apparently.'

'Well, she was a beautiful woman, that's sure. Last year I had the good fortune to visit Berlin, so naturally I took the opportunity of spending a couple of hours in the Egyptian Museum at Charlottenburg, which has *the* famous bust. It was breathtaking. There she was, an isolated exhibit in a room on her own, perfectly lit and lifelike. I half expected her to breathe. And she looked so sophisticated, so glamorous. You would have ...' I paused just in time.

'Yes, I would,' said Philip. 'I would have loved to have seen her. I used to have a poster of her on my bedroom wall when I was young, before I was married, of course,' he added with a smile that suddenly lightened the serious expression that he had when talking.

Liz Kilby came and refilled our glasses. 'I hope you two are going to circulate soon. This is not the Atheneum you know.' She put her hand on Philip's shoulder and whispered, 'I think Laura would like to meet your friend before she turns into a pumpkin.'

'We'll be over in a minute,' Philip said. 'Tell her we have only just started on Akhenaton and Nefertiti.'

We were now so relaxed that I almost made another error by asking him if he had seen a recent television programme on the great pyramid when, to my astonishment, *he* asked me.

Replying that I had, he then said, 'I was very attracted to the theory that after their gods' deaths their spirits left the pyramids to take their pre-appointed place amongst the constellations, to become stars. Rather an attractive idea, don't you think!'

'Yes. If there is any kind of immortality, why not be a star?'

'In fact I think we can be terribly arrogant sometimes in assuming that we know it all. We might be cleverer but are we wiser?'

'Tell me, Philip. How do you follow a television programme when so much of the content is visual?'

'You have to rely on your third eye – your imagination. If it's a good commentary you don't really lose all that much. Pictures are still basically illustrations and if Laura is watching with me she will describe what's on the screen, if it's necessary.'

'And what about astronomy? How on earth do you study the stars if you are blind?'

'You can study anything in braille. And, don't forget, I didn't lose my sight until I was forty-two, so I can still remember a lot of what I saw before then. I know what the constellations look like and where they are at each season of the year. What's the time now?'

I looked at my watch. 'Just coming up to ten-thirty. Why?'

'If we were to step outside now I could point out the exact position of Orion and Sirius, and most of the others – providing it's a clear night.'

'I believe you,' I said. 'But I still find it staggering.'

'And I will tell you another thing that helps. When you are studying astronomy in braille and charting the heavens with your fingertips, you really do feel as if you are touching the stars. It's wonderful … Like an extra sense.'

I stood in amazement and full of admiration. What could I say!

Before I could find the right words, Laura came over with a plate of smoked salmon sandwiches. 'Liz insists that I break up this private little party and get you to mix. Have a sandwich.'

Some people's attractiveness fades the closer they get to one. With Laura it was the reverse. Her beauty came from her personality, from a radiance within that did not rely on cosmetic artistry or a practised social charm. There was an innocent, mischievous look in her eyes when she said to Philip, 'I am going to have this man all to myself for the next twenty minutes, dear, so you go and talk to Susie and Julian. They look as if they need cheering up.'

Philip sighed. 'In that case I shall need my glass re-filling.' He held it towards her. 'Would you mind? You flirt!'

She took his remark as a compliment and said, 'I'm only the sandwich lady, darling. I'll send Keith or someone over to find you in a moment. Off you go!' Then she gently turned him towards the centre of the room. 'They're sitting next to the Christmas tree, on the right-hand side. And be nice to them.'

I watched him as he adroitly wove his way through the rest of the guests without any difficulty. But, why should a mere thirty people be a problem to a man who can find his way among the stars!

Laura took my arm. 'This way,' she said. Although I did not wish a flirtation I couldn't help feeling flattered as we moved slowly towards the door. 'Where are we going?' I asked. 'Carol singing?'

'Sorry to disappoint you, but there's one person here who is dying to meet you. She claims to have read all your books.'

Falling from a great height could not have filled me with more dismay.

20   *A Ballad of the Refugees*

Strip away the legends,
   The angels, shepherds, kings,
     The innocence and glory
       Of which each carol sings;

Forget expensive perfumes,
   Computer-games and food;
     Only by those without
       Is Christmas understood.

A mother without a cot
   In which to lay her child;
     A stable without a door,
       The meagre straw defiled;

A night without a fire,
   A room without a bed;
     No sweetly scented pillow
       On which to rest her head.

No presents for her baby,
   No greetings cards, no wine;
     No lights upon the fir tree,
       No silver stars to shine.

For her the only shelter –
   The corner of a shed;
     The smell of staring cattle
       Waiting to be fed.

Hunger in the morning,
  Hunger still at night;
    Leaner shadows trembling
      In weak candle light.

Refugees, unwanted;
  Burdens on the State.
    Instead of human kindness,
      Humiliation, hate.

In poverty, in sorrow,
  A child came down to earth,
    Alone, unknown, rejected,
      A death more than a birth.

When half the population
  Heard it was God's son,
    They flocked to the manger,
      But the family had gone –

Gone to another country
  To escape Herod's wrath …
    Stripped of that reality
      What are our carols worth?

Yet still we seek to find Him
  With angels, shepherds, kings,
    Longing for the innocence
      Each new birth brings.

21 *The House on the Green*

Hugh had been a builder all his life, as had his father and grandfather, so I was not surprised when he told me that a couple of nights ago he dreamt that he had won a contract to build Thorney Abbey. After all, what are a thousand years to a man who is passionate about local history and can trace his family back for many generations, even to an ancestor – Jourdain le Cave, a retainer who came over with William the Conqueror.

I asked Hugh if, in his dream, he managed to complete the abbey – which was once more than four times its present size. 'Not quite,' he replied, 'it was rather a big job. Perhaps in my next dream I might have finished it, we'll have to see.'

For most of his long life Hugh had lived within a few yards of the abbey and I was sure he would have memories of Christmas that I could add to those I have already collected.

The story will no doubt have echoes of familiarity for many people who can look back over sixty or seventy years to when Christmas was the important family event of the year, other than a wedding.

I will do my best to tell it as it was told to me, though I have taken the liberty of disguising some of the more personal details and have added a word or two to hold the narrative together as a whole; not that my 92-year-old story-teller's account needed much embellishment for he can spin a yarn as well as anyone.

As if to prepare me for whatever drama was to follow he began immediately with the cast:

There was my wife Cecy, Winefride, Josephine, Hugh junior, Uncle Bill, our aunts – Lizzie, Madeline, Trot and Agnes, some brothers-in-law, cousins and four friends from Somerset who had all come to share Christmas with us at 'The House on the Green'. It was the last pre-war Christmas – December 1938 – and seemed to be the final comment on an age that was coming to an end, an age that belonged to the old world rather than the new. The years between the two world wars had not been all that rosy for a lot of people but they still had a quality about them that we have never been able to recapture since 1945. At the same time, most of us felt that a second world war was not very far off and that we should make the most of what peace there was left. Which is why we decided to have the largest family Christmas party we could. By Christmas Eve nineteen of us had gathered together and we began with carol singing round the tree, followed by a cold meat supper.

It was an age in which most firms, large or small, gave gifts of appreciation to their customers. That year, I remember, we received two turkeys and a York ham, which the village baker cooked for us in a rich pastry. Similarly, our own family business had given presents to the people who dealt with us, so the spirit of Christmas was well established by Christmas Eve and any grievances shown during the year were soon forgotten.

There was plenty of activity in the house too. Cecy had made over a hundred mince-pies and we had fourteen pounds of sausages, six Christmas puddings and goodness knows how many cakes and bowls of fruit to see us through the next three or four days.

Because our family name was Cave we decided to decorate the house to look like a cave. There was a long front hall which we covered with sheets of plain paper and then painted so they had the appearance of stones. We then hung a notice outside saying WELCOME TO THE CAVES! I think some of our neighbours thought we were a bit mad at times but we didn't mind. We didn't go much on a dull, ordinary life and always liked to be doing things differently. As Uncle Bill once said, we were uncommonly unpredictable.

As our house was so close to the abbey we all went outside at midnight and waited for the clock to strike twelve. Then we sang *Silent Night, Holy Night.* There was probably a service going on in the abbey for I can remember the lights shining through the stained glass windows. It was an experience you can't forget. The clock could have been chiming the midnight of a thousand years ago because in the moment of silence between each stroke time itself stood still. We, too, could have been a group of people from any century in the village's history preparing to celebrate Christmas. Certainly when we began to sing, our voices sounded strange and distant, as if they no longer belonged to us. It was a bright, starry night and even in the darkness one had a feeling of the great spaces that exist in the Fens. The back of our house looked out over the fields that stretched for forty miles towards the far eastern horizon, and, apart from a few trees that had not been there for more than a hundred years, there was nothing else to be seen. I had the sensation that you get sometimes when waiting for the tide to turn, or for the sun to rise. It was as if the silence of the land knew something of which we, for the time being, were unaware – something that was still hidden from us.

Anyway, we were all awake early on Christmas morning and helped ourselves to breakfast from the choice of meats on the sideboard. Then some of us went for a walk towards Whittlesey Wash to see if there would be any skating during the holidays, and others went to see friends in the village. By eleven o'clock we were all back home, sampling the port or home-made wines, and exchanging more presents. Cecy and the aunts then put the final touches to the traditional Christmas dinner and nineteen happy people gathered round the large table to enjoy what

was, as it turned out, the last such occasion we would all be together. We read from the new books we had been given, participated in the usual games and brought out the annual anecdotes that were always reserved for Christmas.

On Boxing Day we all went in to Peterborough to see the first performance of that year's pantomime, which was a splendid production of *Jack and the*

Beanstalk. It was not only an excellent cast but they also had a very good orchestra. It was wonderful entertainment. Sadly, that theatre closed down years ago and I don't think the pantomimes of today are a patch on those we used to see. They're too noisy and I can't understand why everybody on stage these days needs to have a microphone. Anyway, the total cost of that Christmas was just over two pounds.

And that was that, really. The war that we had been expecting for so long was declared in the September of 1939 and our next few Christmasses were frugal when compared with the one of 1938. Now we all had to have ration-books, clothes-coupons, gas-masks, blackouts, there was a shortage of liquor and quite a lot of our friends had gone off to join the armed services. We also had strangers in the villages now because two searchlight batteries had been camped nearby and the soldiers were frequently marched through the streets as part of their exercises. Naturally when they were off duty they came back to see what the girls were like.

Although there was not to be the usual family gathering for that first war-time Christmas my wife still managed to do some extra baking and took a batch of a hundred mince-pies to each of the two camps. But we had no plum-puddings that year and for a time the custom of local trades-people giving each other Christmas boxes was discontinued. However, I do remember on one occasion getting a bottle of light red wine from the NAAFI in Wisbech, but as it tasted more like red ink it didn't add much to our restricted celebrations.

One thing we all discovered at that time was that it didn't pay to buy anything for cash because if you didn't have a credit account with the shops you often got overlooked when goods were in short supply. Human nature being what it is you can't have a system of ration-books and petrol-coupons without someone trying a fiddle, so there was soon a fair bit of black-market trading going on, even by people who saw themselves as the most honest, virtuous citizens who ever walked the street on Sundays.

By the end of the war, of course, a lot of things had changed. Families had broken up, men had been lost in action, children had grown up with different ideas. Instead of the searchlight units and British soldiers in the street, we now had German prisoners-of-war and even though we were supposed to be at peace again we knew it was going to take a long time to get back to normal, if ever.

We had also left 'The House on the Green' but I can tell you now that never a Christmas passes without I think of the good times we had there all those years ago. When people say 'Christmas is not what it used to be' I know exactly what they mean, and they're right. Clichés can still carry a certain amount of truth and I am jolly grateful that I was able to enjoy something of the old world then.

But, we mustn't get morbid. It's not over yet and I mean to get the most out of what's left. Christmas may be different but it is still Christmas and I have had some very good times during the last twenty years or so. I can remember in 1970 ... but I mustn't keep you any longer, especially as you're in a hurry.

And so this man, who could talk round the clock, or make time stand still, decided to keep the rest of his Christmas memories for another occasion. What happened in 1970, or 1980 is something I shall probably find out when I next go to visit him – unless he's too busy building Thorney Abbey – or dreaming of something even more ambitious – St Paul's Cathedral perhaps?

22 The Arrival of Strangers

1

Brother Penric moved from the writing-desk in the watch-tower where he had been working all afternoon and peered out of the lancet window to the west. Beyond the abbey gates were the small reed-thatched huts of the villagers and a rough track leading into the misty distance.

In his weariness he thought for a moment that he saw two figures approaching, still half a mile away. He rubbed his eyes and looked again. There was nothing. The space of these flat fens diminished everything within eyes' reach. The grey light of the winter afternoon defied any definition of objects, even if they existed. The land was empty and silent, as it always was at this time of the year.

He turned back to his desk and looked at the unfinished manuscript he had been translating. His rush-light was already half-spent. From its measurements he knew it must be past three o'clock. In an hour's time his duty for the day would be over. Then there would be his readings in chapel and at supper. Today, tomorrow, a lifetime.

For the two horsemen making their way towards the abbey there was a different feeling of uncertainty. The light in the east was so close to dusk that the outline of the abbey was no more than a cloud that had settled on the frozen earth. Sometimes it faded so completely into the sky that it appeared, or disappeared, like a mirage.

But, within that abbey, forty-eight Benedictine monks went about their quiet, orderly life, not realizing how frail and insubstantial their building looked on such a day. When Guthlac established the beginnings of the abbey there two hundred years earlier he could not have chosen a more inhospitable spot in the Fens. It was a burden for the mind as well as the body. Yet, out of his simple hermitage had grown this place which was now famous for its library and learning. In summer time scholars from other monasteries made their way here and some of the abbey's manuscripts had already been requested by Rome. In a hundred years' time, what then?

Penric turned back to the narrow window and looked out again. He was certain now that two horsemen were riding towards the abbey. There was movement in the shadows. He rolled his manuscript into its sheath amd waited.

2

Abbot Theodore was pacing up and down in his small study – a square, whitewashed cell on the south side of the cloisters. Apart from his table, a prie-dieu and two wooden chairs, the room was bare. A large crucifix hung on the east wall, his heavy cloak on the back of the door. At fifty-five he was beginning to look an old man. His lined face aged him beyond his years. His tall, lean body stooped at the shoulders and, at the end of the day, weariness was conspicuous in every limb. But he did not grumble. The abbey had been his life's work. There was more than enough to show how successful these years in office had been.

He smiled at the thought, for what is success? Material ambition and jealousy between the abbeys of East Anglia had played too great a part in their lives. With their endowments and revenues the abbots had grown as powerful as kings. Theodore never sought such power. He wanted his abbey to be remembered more for its scholarship than its possessions.

There was a knock at the door. He invited his visitor to enter but when he saw that it was Prior Hugo he sighed heavily. He did not feel like going through the trivial affairs of the day now. He was too tired. The prior stood there, determined and unsmiling. 'Sit down, Hugo. I hope you don't want too much of my time.'

The prior's list of complaints seemed never ending. Brother Ulric had been found asleep in the bakehouse for the second time this month – lazy old man. Brother Oswald had still not repaired the south boundary wall – you could drive twenty hogs through it now. And then something must be done about Brothers Agamund and Grimetukle. They were so senile now they couldn't even stay awake in chapel, let alone work. But they still expected to be fed.

Theodore tried to hide his impatience. 'Don't be too hard on them, Hugo. They have been here a long time. We shall all be old one day, don't let us forget that. I wish you would be more tolerant.'

The prior believed that his task of running the abbey efficiently did not allow for too much tolerance. They had all chosen a life of obedience and service. 'I think we are too easy with all of our brethren, Father, if you will allow me to pass that opinion. Take Brother Penric, for instance. He behaves more like a common troubadour than a servant of Christ. And Brother Brythmer keeps himself so much to himself that one would hardly know that he was here at all.'

'Then you must do something about it, Hugo. Discipline in the abbey is your responsibility, too, isn't it?'

'I do what I can but my responsibilities cover a great many duties these days, it would seem. Perhaps if you spoke to them. You have more authority.'

'Authority? The only authority we have, Hugo, is by example. Surely you know that. What can I do that you cannot? Would it not undermine your authority if I always acted for you? I think it might be more profitable to spend what few minutes I can spare you on discussing the services for Christmas, don't you?'

The prior was unable to disguise his annoyance and clumsily dropped his papers on to the floor.

3

Penric waited until the visitors reached the gates then went down to speak to them. Through the small wooden shutter he saw that the man wore a soldier's tunic and that his fellow traveller was a boy of no more than ten or eleven years. He asked if he could help. They wished to see the abbot. Penric explained that they would be able to see no one now until the morning but were welcome to a bed for the night and a meal.

He opened the gates and invited them in. 'What is the boy's name?'

'Turgar. He was my brother's son.'

'Was?'

'His parents were killed by the Norsemen in the summer when they raided the north-east coast. I promised my brother that I would look after the boy but with my new duties that is becoming increasingly difficult. It's no life for a boy.'

Penric led them into the lower room of the gatehouse and pulled a bell-rope which alerted the refectory.

'I see you are a soldier. Do you have a rank? If so, what do I call you?'

'My name is Edgar and I am a sergeant serving in the northern division of the Mercian Army.'

'How far have you travelled?'

'From the abbey at Repton.'

'Goodness! Then you must be tired and hungry.'

Brother Kenulph entered and Penric asked him if he would arrange for a room to be prepared for their guests and make them a meal. 'The boy looks as if he could sleep on a beanpole.'

Kenulph led them along the dimly lit corridor, up a flight of wooden stairs, into a spacious cell with two mattresses and a table. Above the door hung a large crucifix carved out of black wood.

Turgar began to cry, first with silent tears, then, unable to control his feelings any longer, he sobbed aloud.

'No more tears now, Turgar,' said his uncle. 'Boys of your age don't cry. Tomorrow will be different, you'll see.'

A few moments later there was a quiet tap at the door and Brother Kenulph entered with a tray of bread and salted beef. There was also a jug of wine for Edgar and a jar of goat's milk for the boy. 'Sleep well, my friends. You will be called at five in the morning.'

Turgar drank only half of his milk before falling to sleep

on the mattress. When Edgar had finished his supper he pulled off his boots and lay down on the other bed, staring at the black crucifix above the door. In the flickering taper-light it appeared to throb like burning timber. It reminded him of his brother's house in flames.

The silence of the night began to worry him. He could now understand why people filled up their silences with noise. Noise protected them. In that semi-darkness he felt the walls were about to crush him. What a strange, detached life these monks lived. They closed their gates on the world and knew nothing of the wars, bloodshed, burnings and rape going on in the country. Their nights were spent alone in dark, silent rooms and they were, it seemed, unafraid. His were shared with fellow soldiers who drank their nights away and sang because of fear. And yet this was the place to which he had brought his brother's son who had known nothing but the freedom and daily activities of a busy harbour. What other choice was there? He could not keep the boy with him all winter, not with the men with whom he had to mix each day.

4

Edgar was grateful when there was a knock at the door and Brother Kenulph called them to breakfast. A newly lit fire blazed in the grate beside which stood a large pot of steaming porridge. The smell of it reminded Turgar of his home and his mother. She made good porridge and always believed that a winter day should start with a hot breakfast.

They ate their meal in silence and when they had finished Brother Penric came over to escort them to Abbot Theodore's study.

'You come to us at an unusual time of year,' said Theodore, as he invited them to sit down. 'What brings you to Croyland in the middle of winter?'

'I had no choice, Father. As you can see, I am a soldier and I had to come while my regiment is resting at camp. There will be new campaigns early in the spring and I have to find a place for the boy before then.'

'But why Croyland? Why did you choose to come here when there are excellent monasteries in the north?'

'I am stationed near Repton and when I enquired at the monastery there the Abbot Augustus advised me to bring the boy to you. He said that Turgar would be safer here and well educated.'

'I would like to believe that is true, but is anywhere safe these days? I hear dreadful rumours.'

'I do not think they are rumours, Father.'

'Then tell me what you know, and how you came to be guardian of the boy.'

Edgar gave a brief account of the raids by the Norsemen, how Turgar's village was destroyed, and how he had fled into the woods to escape capture. 'A forester found him and brought him to me, his father's brother. I am fond of the boy but you can understand why I cannot keep him with me when at any minute we might be called to war.'

'War!' sighed Theodore. 'When will it all end? There were wars when I was a young man but they achieved nothing only suffering. What of our abbeys in the north? How many have survived?'

Edgar told him that Durham, Ripon, Whitby and York had all been destroyed.

Theodore shook his head sadly in disbelief. 'But they were all great abbeys, sincere men of God. Why should they be destroyed by these heathen vandals?'

'It is well known, Father, that your abbeys are wealthy places, rich in golden crosses, silver plate and priceless jewels. Those warriors do not worry about your God. For them he does not exist. But your wealth does and for that you are worth plundering.'

'And yet you bring your nephew to us? Why do you suppose that we shall be any safer than those abbeys you have just mentioned?'

'Father Augustus said that your abbey is known more for its learning than its wealth and that you also have the advantage of being more inaccessible in the Fens, surrounded by all these marshlands. I even wondered at one point whether I'd ever find my way here.'

'True. But we are close to a river. If those longships can make their way up our estuaries and rivers then, surely, we are all vulnerable.'

There was a knock at the door and Prior Hugo entered without waiting to be asked. 'I am sorry to interrupt you, Father, but you arranged to discuss the extension to the granary at nine o'clock this morning. We need to plan for an early start in the spring.'

The abbot laughed. 'Spring, Hugo? Who knows what will happen in spring. Here we are, with two days to go before we celebrate Christmas and all you can do is to talk of the work we must do in the spring. We shall probably get six weeks of snow before then, followed by more floods, no doubt.'

'But if you could just approve the proposed layout of the new foundations, then our carpenters will at least be able to start work indoors as soon as Christmas is over.'

Theodore rose reluctantly from his chair. 'Very well, if it's that urgent.' He turned to Edgar. 'I am sorry for this interruption. How soon do you have to get back to your regiment?'

Edgar shrugged his shoulders. 'I have no positive limit on my leave, though I ought not to be away for more than a few days, say three or four.'

'Good. Then why not spend a little more time with us. It will give you the chance of a longer rest and me the opportunity of further conversation with a man of the world, which will be very refreshing!' He put his hand on Edgar's shoulder. 'Now I suppose I had better go and see where the prior wants to put his extensions. Perhaps you would care to join us?'

5

While the abbot and the prior were discussing the plans for the enlarged granary, Edgar and his nephew wandered off to the far side of the cloisters and looked over the wall towards the high bank that protected the abbey from the river.

'Well, what do you think, Turgar? Do you like the

abbey? Could you be happy here?'

Turgar thought for a moment, then said, 'I don't know.'

'You must admit that the food is good and the rest of the monks are kind to us. You would be well educated here and, with a fine education, who knows? You too could go to Rome, or the Holy Land. You could travel, teach, become a scholar. I wish I was your age, I can tell you, with those sort of opportunities.'

'Would I have to stay long?'

Edgar hesitated. 'That depends on how well you study, how you behave yourself, and what you want to do with your life when you are grown up.'

'I might decide to be a soldier like you, then I wouldn't have to learn too much, would I.'

'Don't you be so sure. An educated soldier fares better than an uneducated one. Besides, Turgar, you'll never make a soldier.'

'But if I have to stay here, when shall I see you again?'

Edgar put his arm round the boy. 'How can I answer that? Just believe me, Turgar, it's the best thing for you – at least for the next few years.'

They walked back along the river-bank in silence. A cold wind blew in from the east and they watched twelve wild geese fly in to settle on the marshes.

Then from the far corner of the cloisters they could hear the monotonous clanging of the chapel bell calling the order to their next service. It was a hard, metallic sound that reminded Edgar of a blacksmith's hammer striking an anvil. From every section of the abbey monks emerged in twos and threes to make their way to chapel.

Abbot Theodore came over to speak to them. 'I am afraid, sergeant, that bell governs our lives. We are ruled by a timetable of prayer, thank goodness, so I must ask you to excuse me again for three-quarters of an hour. You may come to chapel if you wish but if you would rather have more time to yourselves then you are at liberty to explore wherever you like. We have nothing to hide. Perhaps we could meet in my study at noon. I will ask Brother Penric to show Turgar our wonderful library, then we can talk about things. All right?'

Edgar watched the tall, stooping figure of the abbot glide quickly through the cloisters even though he had a slight limp. It was like watching a shadow with a purpose.

6

The two men met again at midday as planned. Theodore poured a goblet of wine and handed it to his guest. 'Tell me, Edgar, a little more about yourself. Have you always been a soldier? Is it something you enjoy?'

'Enjoyment doesn't come into it, Father. It is a duty, as yours is. I believe that the country needs protecting and the stronger we make our armies the better chance we have of living in peace. We have to be able to match force with force. It is always the weak who suffer.'

'That is one way of looking at it, I suppose. But you will understand why I cannot share your views. I am a man of peace, not fear. Violence, to me, is immoral and barbaric. There must be a better way.'

He poured more wine. 'Tell me more about what happened to Turgar's family. What did you say his father was?'

'A harbour-master, just north of the Humber. When the Norsemen attacked him that morning they demanded of him one hundred pieces of gold, a sum of money he would not have seen, let alone possess. So they burnt down his house and then those of his neighbours and took what they could. His wife was expecting her third child and you don't need me to describe what happened to her – and all the other women in the village.'

'How much of this did the boy see?'

'I cannot say. I think he must have run off in terror almost immediately, otherwise they would have caught him and taken him back with them. He was probably with his father when the attackers landed and went to raise the alarm. He knows what happened all right, which is why he is always talking about getting his revenge. You know what young boys are like.'

Theodore managed a half smile. 'You say that your brother's wife was expecting her third child. What became of the one other than Turgar?'

'I don't know that either. She was two years younger than her brother and although I searched the ruins of the village for her I could find no trace. She might possibly be alive somewhere, but I doubt it. You must understand, Father, that we have seen things like this many times.'

Theodore rubbed his lean hands over his face. 'You are indeed a bringer of bad tidings, sergeant.'

'Perhaps you can understand now why I am a soldier.'

Theodore put his empty goblet back on the table. 'And you should now understand why I am a priest. Peace! We must have peace.'

'I agree, but that is an ideal state which can never be achieved through weakness. From what little I know about history it would appear that there have always been wars, and always will be. It's part of human nature.'

The abbot walked over towards his window and looked across the cloisters. Then he turned round and spoke to Edgar. 'Have you finished your wine? Then I would like you to come with me.'

The abbot led his guest towards the chapel, opened the door and stood back for him to enter. The white walls reflected the cold winter light which still shone through the south windows. The decorations were simple rather than ostentatious. Two large candlesticks and a heavy golden cross stood on the altar which had an embroidered frontal cloth in the design of two peacocks. 'They are a symbol of everlasting life,' said Theodore. Painted on the wall behind the altar were the words of Saint Benedict:

Prefer nothing to the love of Christ:
Bear persecution for the sake of justice:
The first degree of humility is obedience.

The abbot read them slowly in a quiet voice. 'I have lived by those words, sergeant. If I gave my blessing to war, or agreed with it as the only solution to our quarrels, I would be guilty of war. I am convinced that one day, when men are more civilized, they will be able to sit down and reason out their differences, don't you?'

Edgar remained silent.

The abbot said:

Please, please do not think I am condemning you for what you are now. There is in human nature a very thin crust between passivity and violence, between good and evil, right and wrong. There is an element of cruelty in us all, which is why we must learn to control it. Equally, I believe there is a capacity in all of us to love, which is why we must learn how to use it. I am delighted that you can spend a few days with us, especially at this time of the year as we prepare to celebrate Christ's Mass.

Edgar knew very little of the Christian faith or the Church's calendar of festivities. Had he stayed at camp he would have been celebrating with his comrades the returning of light to the earth after the winter solstice. That would have had no religious significance other than the rebirth of life in grass, forests and fields; the start of another season of mating among bird, beast and man; the promise that it would be spring and that soldiers could once again sleep under the stars.

As the two men walked away from the chapel Theodore

said to Edgar, 'Now that you know a little more about us do you still want me to take your nephew as a young postulant?'

Before he could reply he felt the abbot's hand grip firmly on his wrist. 'You do not have to answer now. We will talk about it again after supper.'

7

The refectory was glowing warmly with candle-light and the flames of a huge fire. Baskets of seasoned logs stood near the hearth and the smell of apple-wood smoke drifted across the tables where the men sat waiting for the meal to begin.

Theodore received his dish, took his share of bread, then lifted the silver goblet of wine to his lips as if to drink before saying grace. As he did so he noticed the flames of the fire reflecting in his cup; warmth and light held together at the same time in his hands. Yes, he had achieved much since taking charge of Croyland but there was still much more to do. He should not have been so short with Prior Hugo about the plans for next spring.

The rest of the community waited. It was unlike the abbot to daydream so long before the commencement of a meal. Had he forgotten the grace? Hugo leaned forward and quietly coughed. Theodore looked up, smiled his apology, then asked the customary blessing on their food.

Whilst the brethren ate in silence, Brother Penric stood at the lectern and began reading from his new translation of the gospels:

*And it came to pass in those days that there went out
a decree from Caesar Augustus that all the world should
be taxed … And all went to be taxed, every one to his
own city. And Joseph also went up from Galilee,
out of the city of Nazareth, into Judea, unto the
city of David, which is called Bethlehem … to be
taxed with Mary his espoused wife, being great with
child …*

Edgar listened to the rich, clear voice that was speaking in a language he could understand. He had heard parts of the bible read before but it was always in Latin, or Greek, and the words meant nothing to him. But Penric's words had a majesty that made every sentence shine with meaning:

And so it was, that, while they were there, the days
were accomplished that she should be delivered. And
she brought forth her first-born son and wrapped him
in swaddling clothes, and laid him in a manger, because
there was no room for them in the inn ...

Theodore also listened, although he had heard the story many times before, even in the Holy Land itself, there was always something more to learn from it and the new language gave it a striking immediacy and freshness. As in all good stories one wanted to know what happened next:

And there were in the same country shepherds abiding
in the field, keeping watch over their flock by night.
And, lo, the angel of the Lord came upon them, and the
glory of the Lord shone round about them; and they were
sore afraid. And the angel said unto them; Fear not,
for, behold, I bring you tidings of great joy, which
shall be to all people ...

Penric finished his reading and soon the meal was over. Theodore slowly drained his goblet and held it for a moment in his hands to see if it would again reflect the fire's light. But the flames had died down and there was only a dark glow in the embers.

He asked his prior to say the grace and then the community dispersed to its quarters. Edgar took Turgar back to their room and explained that he now had to see Abbot Theodore in his study. Turgar knew what that meeting would decide.

8

The following morning a thick mist lay over the Fens and it was difficult to imagine that there was anything else out there in the silent world.

Edgar was grateful that he did not have to start his journey back to his regiment today. He woke Turgar and told him to get up.

Already the abbey was set on its daily order of services that never changed – Matins, Lauds, Prime, Terce, Sext, None, Vespers and Compline. 'The more order you have in your life,' the abbot said frequently, 'the less room there is for disorder.'

Theodore met his guests as they walked towards the refectory. 'Good-morning, my friends! It's not very cheerful weather for Christmas Eve, is it! But then I do not for one moment suppose it should be. We must make up for it by the warmth of our spirits. You will, I trust, be joining with us in a celebration of our midnight Mass?'

Edgar promised that he and Turgar would be there. His few meetings with the abbot had impressed him greatly. He was a wise, gentle, but strong person whose faith was unshaken. He was both a traditionalist who respected the past and a visionary who wished to shape the future, because it was only the future that he could influence. He was a peace-lover and a man who believed in enlightenment. He would never understand Edgar's belief in military power.

The day was now making the soldier feel trapped. There was nothing more to do, nothing to see, nowhere to go. The walls of the abbey closed in on him even worse than the mist. Waiting is always difficult, for a man of action. He counted the service bells. He watched the sky darken. He saw the candles being lit throughout the dormitories – little squares of yellow light that helped to console his loneliness.

Then, after supper, the slow procession of the monks again making their way to the chapel, each robed specially for Christmas Eve, all of them chanting as they went, their lanterns flickering in the night air, like glow-worms. Edgar and Turgar followed.

The chapel was brightly lit and smelt of incense. Although he did not understand all that was going on he recognized both the solemnity and joy of the service.

Once again Brother Penric was responsible for the readings and Edgar was impressed even more by the power and beauty of his words:

And it came to pass, as the angels were gone away from them into heaven, the shepherds said one to another, let us now go even unto Bethlehem and see this thing which is come to pass, which the Lord hath made known unto us. And they went with haste, and found Mary and Joseph, and the baby lying in a manger. And when they had seen it, they made known abroad the saying which was told them concerning the child. And all they that heard it wondered at those things which were told them by the shepherds. But Mary kept all these things and pondered them in her heart ...

Edgar believed that he was listening to words that would last for a thousand years. He could feel them working inside him like red wine warming the stomach. They also brought him a feeling of peace that surpassed all the glories of battle. And at that moment his regiment felt like something that belonged to an unreal world, to a forgotten time. He was not sure now how much he wanted to return to a life that might not survive beyond his next fight.

He looked at his young nephew. What would his future be like? He had not had to make any decisions yet. The Norsemen had seen to that. The child sat there now in a state of wonder rather than fear, his large eyes shining, his face radiant with all that was happening. Were the burning houses of his father's harbour already beginning to dim in his memory?

The brothers returned from the communion table to their stalls and knelt in silence. Then, in a loud voice, Abbot Theodore cried out:

Benedictus qui venit in nomine Domini.
Hosanna in excelsis ...

The congregation rose and replied *Hosanna in excelsis!* Turgar rose with them. Perhaps another choice had been made for him. If so, Edgar was both grateful and envious. When the time came for him to leave he would go knowing that he had done all he could for his charge.

9

It was not until the afternoon of Christmas Day that Abbot Theodore sent for Turgar and his uncle. He greeted them warmly and asked them to sit down.

He spoke first to the boy. 'Well, young man, have you enjoyed your visit?'

'Yes, Father.'

'Then how would you like to stay with us a little longer? I have been talking to your uncle and I am sure you must know why he has brought you to us.'

Turgar nodded.

'We could teach you to read and write Latin and Greek, like Brother Penric. You would learn how to illuminate books, or how to compose chants. Or, should those subjects not appeal to you, you could work in the gardens and become a herbalist, or you could be a skilled craftsman and carpenter. This great building is always in need of repair and improvement, as my prior keeps telling me … Personally I would like to see you become a scholar, able to enrich the minds of other men. What do you say?'

'Does that mean I would have to become a monk for the rest of my life?'

'Only when you are older, and ready. You would become a postulant first and receive instruction to prepare you for that life. Such decisions are not taken lightly and you will need guidance. But there is plenty of time.'

'Will my uncle be allowed to visit me if I stay?'

'Eventually. We are not a closed community and are always pleased to see our friends. But you would need to settle down first and it is our custom not to allow our postulants any visitors for a year. Then, if your studies are satisfactory and you have been obedient, your uncle may see you.'

Theodore turned to Edgar. 'Do you wish to say anything further?'

'Only that we are extremely grateful to you, Father, for the kindness you have shown and the offer you have made. For my part I do not think my nephew could be in a better place and, if you are prepared to accept him, then I know he will do his best to please you.'

'Good, then that is settled. You, I imagine, are now anxious to get back to your wars, eh?' said Theodore with a smile.

'Tomorrow, if the weather permits.'

'Then you must eat a good supper this evening. I will ask our cellarer to choose some of our best wines in your honour.'

10

Edgar woke early, put on his leather tunic, his kilt and sword-belt before eating the breakfast that had been prepared for him. He looked at Turgar who was still asleep and was uncertain as to whether he should wake him or not. Then, feeling it would be unkind to the boy to leave without saying goodbye, he gently shook him until he roused.

'I have to go now, Turgar. Are you coming to see me off?'

Turgar sat up and rubbed his eyes.

'No tears, now,' said Edgar. 'Remember the good name of your parents and do as you are told by the brethren. I will be back next spring to see how you are progressing. And don't forget to look after your horse.'

Turgar put on his cloak and followed his uncle out into the cloisters. When they reached the main gates Brother Kenulph was waiting for them with Edgar's horse. 'He has been groomed and fed, sergeant, and here is a small hamper of food for you. May God go with you.'

Edgar put his hand on Turgar's shoulder and said to Kenulph. 'You will look after him, won't you, and see that he is brought up to be a good man, like his father.'

'Have no fears. We shall be like a family to him. When you come to see him in a year's time you will hardly know him. He will be a fine young man.'

Edgar was just going to mount his horse when he heard Abbot Theodore's voice: 'Sergeant! I cannot let you go, my friend, without my blessing. I have enjoyed your company and shall look forward to your bringing me better news when you visit us again. May God keep you from harm even more than you hope to keep us.'

The two men shook hands and Brother Kenulph opened the gates for Edgar to begin his journey back to camp. As Turgar watched him ride out into the cold shadows of that winter morning his thoughts went back to the day when his uncle became his guardian, to the day when his true home lay in ashes and his parents had been taken from him.

11

The following spring, as the abbey began its Easter celebrations, three long-boats slowly made their way up-river as far as they could. Against the early morning light and grey mist the carved heads of a raven, dragon and snake could be seen on the prows as they inched their way past the reeds. When the oarsmen could no longer row, the first and last members of the crews poled their crafts towards a mooring-place. The only sounds that came from the boats were the clicking of buckles as tunics and helmets were fastened and shields were lifted from the boats' sides. No one spoke. The men still waited for a signal. They knew that their success would again depend on surprise and swiftness of attack.

Less than a mile away they could see the shadowy outline of the abbey where the daily services had already begun. It was Good Friday and the monks were now assembling for Prime. Brother Ulric lit new candles. Brother Wilfrid rekindled the incense burner. Abbot Theodore walked solemnly to his chair. The rest of the community took their places in the choir stalls and pews. Everything was as it should be. The responses were made without hesitation:

Kyrie eleison.　Kyrie eleison.　Kyrie eleison.
Christe eleison.　Christe eleison.

Along the river-bank sixty Norsemen now moved purposefully forward, their reindeer-skin boots swishing through the tall wet grass, their shields brushing against the hawthorn bushes already in leaf. All carried swords, axes or daggers. Some had torches soaked in oil, ready to be lit from their leader's taper.

They reached the abbey walls and entered the cloisters. Soon all torches were lit and the men ran towards the chapel, shattering the devotion of those within as the doors burst open.

Theodore saw them first and cried out, 'Have mercy upon us, Lord. Have mercy!' Then he turned and fell on his knees at the altar, imploring God to protect them on this holy day of sacrifice.

His plea went unheeded. As the monks tried to escape they were axed down. The blood ritual had begun. There was only one end. As Theodore lifted his head to look up at the figure of Christ on the cross a soldier's sword pierced his head. The prior rushed to save him but was beaten to the ground.

Soon all the buildings were alight – the chapel, library, dormitories and granary. The wood crackled as the flames spread. Black smoke desecrated the sky.

The only two people to escape were Brother Penric and Turgar who had gone down into the village to deliver the abbot's annual Easter gift of pace-eggs to the children. But now the villagers hid in terror fearing that the Norsemen would soon attack them.

Four miles away, in the abbey at Thorney, some of the monks could already see the fire rising from the ruins of Croyland. Would it be their turn next? The day and night passed without incident and the following morning several of them rode over to see for themselves what had happened. The atrocities were worse than they had imagined. Many of the bodies were charred beyond recognition. Those who could be buried separately, were. The remains of the rest were put into a mass grave and prayers said for them.

Before the summer, and with the help of the villagers, the ruined cloisters had been cleared of debris and a stone cross was erected in memory of all the brethren who had died. It stood where Abbot Theodore had been murdered at the altar steps. Into its base had been carved the one word: RESURGAM.

What had become of Penric and Turgar no one knew.

12

Many years later, people who were only children in the village when the abbey was destroyed, saw a tired monk walking towards the gate where the watch-tower had stood. Their children, who still used the abbey ruins for their games, followed him. Inside the cloisters he stood, uncertain of where he wanted to be. There he noticed the stone cross. He walked slowly, as if in procession, and knelt down before it, praying in words the children could not understand.

When he had finished one of the boys said, 'Who are you?'

'I am Brother Edgar!' he replied. 'And who are you?'

The girls giggled among themselves. Then one of them said, 'There was another man here the other week but he wasn't as old as you.' And another added, 'He had all his hair on … And a beard.'

Edgar's face changed from sorrow to joy and then to puzzlement. 'Do you know where he came from, or where he went?'

They shook their heads and Edgar was disappointed that they could not tell him more. His thoughts went back to that Christmas Day when he sat in the abbot's study discussing Turgar's future. He still wanted to believe that they had made the right decision, despite all that had happened for, surely, the boy had not perished, or forgotten. It must have been his nephew who had also returned. But from which abbey had he made his pilgrimage?

He looked at the children again who had been silently watching him. 'Did the man you speak of wear a brown cloak like mine?'

They shook their heads. Then one of the boys said, 'He

was a soldier. He had a sword.'

'Are you sure?' asked Edgar, as the lightness of his heart gave way to doubt.

All the children agreed that their friend's statement was true. The man was a soldier in a blue coat with gold stripes and did have a sword.

'He did what you just did. He went and knelt at that cross. Why did he do that?'

Edgar was now certain who it must have been. But, sadly, for Turgar the need for revenge had been stronger than his ability to forgive. So why had he come back? Could Abbot Theodore's example, perhaps, still speak to him from beyond the grave?

Suddenly the children turned and ran away, as if afraid, as if they had just seen another figure standing in the shadows of a clump of willow trees which grew where the library had once been.

Edgar let them go, grateful to be left alone. One task above all others became clear to him then. The abbey at Croyland must rise again, greater than even Theodore had dreamed.

23   *The Road Back*

I would go
When no one was looking,
When the embroidered robes
Had been given to the poor
And the smell of cattle dung
Had mixed with frankincense and myrrh.

I would go
While the priests were feasting
And soldiers cleaned their guns;
While Herod's shells were silent
And Wise Men still following
The star's path through the firmament.

I would go
When, on desolate roads,
The crippled children came
Bringing their gifts of crutches
To the child they could not name –
Stripped like them of this world's riches.

I would go
While the mother rested
After her first agony,
And there, in the shadows, stand
Gazing at the makeshift bed –
One question burning in my mind.

I would go
In the steps of an old
Woman who, through the crowd,
Touched the hem of his garment,
Knowing that her hand once held
Unseen, life's greatest sacrament.

I would go
As a shy shepherd boy,
As a prodigal son
Wanting to begin again;
As one under a night sky
Waiting for love to fall, like rain.

24　Twelve Days Wonder

At the beginning of this book I explained how Christmas often began for me in August, when I worked for the local education authority and had to plan the schools' carol services in the middle of summer. So I find it something of a coincidence that I come to these final pages in the summer of many years later, with the temperatures again close to a heatwave and most of the nation relaxing in the sun.

Admittedly I am no longer playing carols on the piano to the bewilderment of my neighbours and I do not have to decide which nine lessons will be read in the cathedral this year. Even so, having spent so much of my time thinking about 'bleak mid-winters' and other people's celebrations, it is still disconcerting to look up from my desk and see a vast sky shimmering with heat. Instead of putting more logs on the fire, I open another window. As I do so, the thought occurs to me that these are the conditions in which thousands of people in other parts of the world actually have to spend their Christmasses.

I have some friends in Brisbane, for instance, who will be having their Christmas dinner on a beach, in temperatures of eighty-plus, with a warm sea lapping in from the coral reef. But it will still be a 'traditional Christmas' for them with roast turkey, presents, and even carols. 'You'd be surprised,' they say, 'what a few Christmas cards with robins, stage-coaches and Yule logs can do for you.' Nearby, families set up their tents for Christmas Day with their relatives and friends. Picnic hampers appear and Santa Claus will more than likely arrived in red swimming-trunks and on water-skis rather than on a sleigh.

But I have to admit that I was always pleased when my summer Christmasses progressed to the reality of December as I would find it difficult to celebrate the season in any other climate of the year.

What has been confirmed for me during the many conversations that I have had with other people in the Fens during the last few months is that Christmas still does mean something to them, whether the children are grown up or not. For some it may have little to do with religious beliefs but the true spirit is seldom far away, however much they try to disguise it. Goodwill and generosity survive – as many charity organizations can prove, and in most hearts old loves are rekindled, or affirmed.

Understandably, Christmas for a lot of us is still inextricably bound up with our childhoods and it is only as children that we can fully enjoy the magic and make-believe of its appeal. Nearly everyone I talked with spoke of what Christmas was like for them when they were children, no matter how poor they had been, or how privileged. It was an annual event that mattered and one that left a lasting impression long after the tinsel had faded.

It will always be so – I hope.

Although the shops may now be competing with my former early starts to Christmas there is, of course, an official beginning and an official end to the festivities. The twelve days of Christmas have inspired several legends, poems, and at least one famous carol, which is especially popular with choirs.

I have never had the pleasure of receiving a partridge in a pear tree or three French hens, and certainly not eight maids a-milking or eleven ladies dancing. For me the Christmas season is well and truly over by the time I attend the Epiphany service held each year in the little Puritan Chapel at Guyhirn, near Wisbech. This small, simple, rectangular place of worship, with its strong links with the Huguenots, is unique to the Fens. Above the entrance door is a stone bearing the date 1660, more significant perhaps as the year which became a turning point in English history, when this country ceased to be a commonwealth and reverted to the monarchy with the accession of Charles II. In spite of, or perhaps because of, its simplicity the Chapel has a wonderful atmosphere of peace. It sits like a stranded boat beached on the shores of history, holding the past and the present together in a very real sense of continuity and belonging. One is made movingly aware of all that has gone before and of how important each present moment is to the future as well as ourselves. Because there is no artificial lighting or heating, the services held there throughout the year are few, sometimes no more than three or four. I enjoy them all, especially the afternoon Service of Epiphany in January when the plain building with its stark pews is candle-lit and the surrounding landscape begins to fade into dusk. One needs to remember such moments as a protection against less peaceful times:

> You are an ark through which light shines
> On certain afternoons,
> When winter settles like a bird
> Upon the silent Fens.
>
> Within your walls the silence heals
> And, as the candles glow,
> We hear of love, of birth, and watch
> The Wise Men come and go.
>
> You are an ark from which light shines
> When darkness gathers round,
> A point of stillness in a world
> Battered by violent sound.
>
> Stay firm, stay constant and withstand
> (As Noah's house before,)
> The threat of floods, the storm-clouds which
> Now hover at your door.

You are an ark in which light shines
For all who come to pray
Within the simple setting of
Each year's Epiphany.

Flames have no shadows as they burn
On window-sill and stone.
Here, where the year begins again,
Truth and light are one.

So twelve days of wonder come to an end. We may sigh with relief and say, never again, grateful to be released from all the excesses of turkey, drinks, social gatherings and games. We shall probably be eager to take down the decorations and the cards, to throw out the shrivelled evergreen and get back to normal. Or we shall feel sorry that our cosy escape from routine and reality is over, that tomorrow we must step out again into the world as it is. We may be poorer, or richer, more secure or afraid. For a few weeks the next Christmas will seem an age away and, for all we know, it will be different.

What most of us will try to do, I suppose, is to make it almost the same because we need to hang on to something, whether true or make-believe. For whatever reason I would like to think that the season brings out the best in us, as it did in Scrooge, and that must mean something.